www.prolancewriting.com
California, USA

Edited by Hadeer Sahar Soliman, Esq.

©2017 Islam4families.com
ISBN-13: 978-0-9962457-3-9
Printed in USA

A SPECIAL THANK YOU

A special thanks to my dad for initiating the research about the story of Musa in the Quran, allowing this book to tell the story in sequence.

PREFACE

In 1998, when Christmas, Hanukkah, and Ramadan were all celebrated during the month of December, I took my three children, then 9-year-old Hadeer, 8-year-old Siraj and 6-year-old Janna to Story Time at the local library.

With great excitement, the librarian told the wide-eyed children that she would read to them stories about the holidays taking place in December: Christmas and Hanukkah.

My daughter, Hadeer, almost automatically, said to me, "How about Ramadan, Mommy? That's in December, too."

After Story Time was over, I asked the librarian to share with the children a story about Ramadan because the holidays coincided this year.

The librarian responded, "Ramadan is not a fun month; it's religious."

I proceeded to tell her that, like Christmas and Hanukkah, Ramadan is also a religious time, and that it can, in fact, be fun, just like those two holidays.

After a long discussion on this matter, the librarian agreed. If I could bring her a children's story about Ramadan, she would share it during Story Time at the library.

Naturally, I looked in the library for a children's short story about Ramadan.

However, to my children's disappointment and mine, there were none.

That is when I began working with my children on building on their own experiences to write a story about Ramadan.

I also designed an art project for the children to participate in during Story Time the following week at the library.

Alhamdulilah, we were ready that week with a story to share with the children, and we made a lantern as the library's art project for the week.

The following year, when I started teaching and developing the Islamic Studies curriculum at New Horizon School in Los Angeles, Calif., I asked my students to write short stories about Ramadan.

I also requested that they write poems about the Quran, Ramadan, Eid, the Prophet Mohammad (pbuh), and thankfulness.

I then worked on developing creative art projects to bring to life Islamic ideals and help us celebrate Islamic holidays.

Not only did we relate existing arts and crafts projects to Islam, but we also created new ideas and taught the students to relate everything we used to the One who created the materials: Allah. We taught them that all man-made items are ultimately natural creations by Allah's.

As an example, we asked the students what wax is made of and encouraged them to do their research and come back to class with an answer. "

Wax is made from natural things like cattle fat, sugars, and honey," they wrote. Then we asked them what people use wax for. "People use wax for things like crayons, candles, and cosmetics," they'd answer. We wanted to clarify to the students that by using their creativity and Allah's creations, they could produce beautiful art!

Then, from 2011 to 2017, I worked with a designer and editor to publish children's books. I developed five books for children: Ramadan Stories, Islamic Poems, Islamic Arts & Crafts Projects, All About Allah, and All About Prophet Musa. They are available at:

www.islam4families.com

I hope my story will encourage other parents to work with their local communities to inspire their children to be proud of and to use their resources to develop their Muslim American identities.

~ Sahar Abdel-Aziz

3

TABLE OF CONTENTS:

INTRODUCTION

The Quran, the holy book of Muslims, is full of stories about people in our history. It casts light upon many personalities such as messengers and prophets, including Prophets Muhammad (peace be upon him), Isa, and Nooh, just to name a few. One of the most written about, however, is Prophet Musa. Allah gives many details in the Quran about his birth, adulthood, revelation, and his deliverance with the Israelites from Egypt. We learn lessons from his life and prophethood.

CHAPTER 1
PROPHET MUSA'S BIRTH

Prophet Musa was born in Egypt in 1393 BCE (before the common era).

His family's name was Imran, and he was born into a family of Israelites.

Israelites are members of the tribes of Israel, who we also know as the descendants of Prophet Yacub.

They originally lived in a city named Canaan, but they spread all around the Near East, including Egypt.

Musa was born during a time when the Israelites were slaves to the Egyptian Pharaoh, who was brutal and oppressed them, forcing them to live under very harsh circumstances. There are many Quranic verses that tell just how terrible the Pharaoh was.

> Allah says, Pharaoh exalted himself in the land, and divided its people into factions. He persecuted a group of them, slaughtering their sons, while sparing their daughters. He was truly a corrupter. (28:4)

> إِنَّ فِرْعَوْنَ عَلَا فِى الْأَرْضِ وَجَعَلَ أَهْلَهَا شِيَعًا يَسْتَضْعِفُ طَائِفَةً مِّنْهُمْ يُذَبِّحُ أَبْنَاءَهُمْ وَيَسْتَحْىِ نِسَاءَهُمْ ۚ إِنَّهُ كَانَ مِنَ الْمُفْسِدِينَ (28:4)

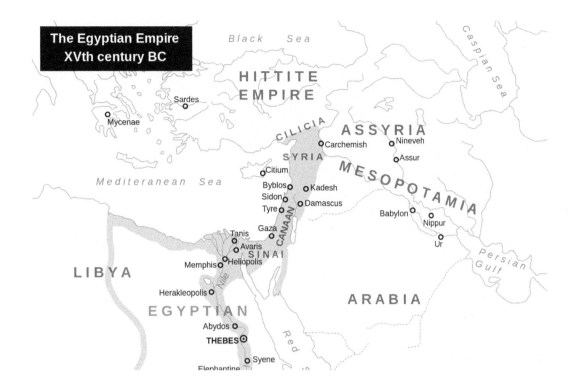

The 28th Surah of the Quran, "The Stories," is full of details about Prophet Musa and his life. It starts by mentioning Pharaoh's oppression of the Israelites, and details the birth of Musa and his early life. It tells of when Musa received Allah's message as an adult, and his conflicts with Pharaoh. There are more than 400 verses throughout the Quran that tell us about Musa's life.

Before Musa was born, Pharaoh had a dream about a fire that burnt everything in his kingdom. The fire in his dream came from Jerusalem. His priests interpreted this dream to mean that the fall of the Pharaoh would be brought about by a boy from the Israelites.

Pharaoh ordered the killing of all newborn Israelite males. His advisers said killing the male infants of the Israelites would result in a loss of manpower and suggested instead that they should be killed one year and spared the next. Musa was born in the year in which infants were to be killed.

When Musa was born, his mother feared for his life. She received inspiration from Allah to put Musa in a chest in the Nile.

> Allah says, We inspired the mother of Musa, "Nurse him; then, when you fear for him, cast him into the river, and do not fear, nor grieve; We will return him to you, and make him one of the messengers." (28:7)

Musa's mother is one of two mothers who received inspiration from Allah; Isa's mother is the other. Both women received inspiration about their children, who later became prophets. Although Musa's mother feared leaving him in the river, she trusted Allah's promise.

وَأَوْحَيْنَآ إِلَىٰٓ أُمِّ مُوسَىٰٓ أَنْ أَرْضِعِيهِ فَإِذَا خِفْتِ عَلَيْهِ فَأَلْقِيهِ فِى ٱلْيَمِّ وَلَا تَخَافِى وَلَا تَحْزَنِىٓ إِنَّا رَآدُّوهُ إِلَيْكِ وَجَاعِلُوهُ مِنَ ٱلْمُرْسَلِينَ (28:7)

Allah says, *When We inspired your mother, saying, Put your child into the chest, then place him in the river. Let the river wash him onto its bank, and he will be taken in by an enemy of Mine and his, "I showered you with My love and planned that you should be brought up under My watchful eye.* (20:38-39)

إِذْ أَوْحَيْنَا إِلَىٰ أُمِّكَ مَا يُوحَىٰ ٣٨ أَنِ ٱقْذِفِيهِ فِى ٱلتَّابُوتِ فَٱقْذِفِيهِ فِى ٱلْيَمِّ فَلْيُلْقِهِ ٱلْيَمُّ بِٱلسَّاحِلِ يَأْخُذْهُ عَدُوٌّ لِّى وَعَدُوٌّ لَّهُ ۚ وَأَلْقَيْتُ عَلَيْكَ مَحَبَّةً مِّنِّى وَلِتُصْنَعَ عَلَىٰ عَيْنِىَ ٣٩
(20:38-39)

Musa's mother told his sister to follow the chest to watch over Musa. As she followed the chest along the riverbank, Musa was discovered by the Pharaoh's wife, Asiyah. She took him out of the river and convinced the Pharaoh to adopt him. Asiyah then ordered the wet nurses to nurse Musa, but he wouldn't nurse.

When Musa's sister saw that he wasn't feeding, she informed the Pharaoh that she knew a woman who could feed Musa. The Pharaoh ordered her to bring this woman to his kingdom. So she brought her mother and he appointed her Musa's wet nurse. And that's how Musa was reunited with his mother and sister, while Pharaoh did not know of their actual identities. Allah's promise to Musa's mom came true in this moment.

Allah says, *The heart of Musa's mother became vacant. She was about to disclose him, had We not steadied her heart, that she may remain a believer. She said to his sister, "Trail him." So she watched him from afar, and they were unaware. We forbade him breastfeeding at first. So she said, "Shall I tell you about a family that can raise him for you, and will look after him?" Thus We returned him to his mother, that she may be comforted, and not grieve, and know that God's promise is true. But most of them do not know.* (28:10-13)

وَأَصْبَحَ فُؤَادُ أُمِّ مُوسَىٰ فَٰرِغًا ۖ إِن كَادَتْ لَتُبْدِى بِهِ لَوْلَآ أَن رَّبَطْنَا عَلَىٰ قَلْبِهَا لِتَكُونَ مِنَ ٱلْمُؤْمِنِينَ ١٠ وَقَالَتْ لِأُخْتِهِ قُصِّيهِ ۖ فَبَصُرَتْ بِهِ عَن جُنُبٍ وَهُمْ لَا يَشْعُرُونَ ١١ وَحَرَّمْنَا عَلَيْهِ ٱلْمَرَاضِعَ مِن قَبْلُ فَقَالَتْ هَلْ أَدُلُّكُمْ عَلَىٰ أَهْلِ بَيْتٍ يَكْفُلُونَهُ ۥ لَكُمْ وَهُمْ لَهُ ۥ نَٰصِحُونَ ١٢ فَرَدَدْنَٰهُ إِلَىٰ أُمِّهِ كَىْ تَقَرَّ عَيْنُهَا وَلَا تَحْزَنَ وَلِتَعْلَمَ أَنَّ وَعْدَ ٱللَّهِ حَقٌّ وَلَٰكِنَّ أَكْثَرَهُمْ لَا يَعْلَمُونَ ١٣
(28:10-13)

Tests of Musa's prophethood came throughout his life. While playing on Pharaoh's lap as a child, Musa grabbed the Pharaoh's beard. Pharaoh wondered if Musa might be the Israelite who would overthrow him, and decided to kill him.

Pharaoh's wife pleaded with him, arguing that Musa was just a baby. But Pharaoh wasn't convinced. So he decided to test Musa, placing two plates in front of him, one with rubies and the other with hot, glowing coals. Musa reached for the rubies, but Angel Gabriel directed his hand toward the coals. So Musa grabbed a glowing coal and put it inside his mouth, burning his tongue. Convinced Musa was no longer a threat, Pharaoh decided to spare his life. But Musa would suffer a speech impairment for the rest of his life.

> **Allah says,** Pharaoh's household picked him up, to be an opponent and a sorrow for them. Pharaoh, Hamaan, and their troops were sinners. Pharaoh's wife said, "An eye's delight for me and for you. Do not kill him; perhaps he will be useful to us, or we may adopt him as a son." But they did not foresee. (28:8-9)

فَٱلْتَقَطَهُ ءَالُ فِرْعَوْنَ لِيَكُونَ لَهُمْ عَدُوًّا وَحَزَنًا إِنَّ فِرْعَوْنَ وَهَـٰمَـٰنَ وَجُنُودَهُمَا كَانُواْ خَـٰطِـِينَ ٨ وَقَالَتِ ٱمْرَأَتُ فِرْعَوْنَ قُرَّتُ عَيْنٍ لِّى وَلَكَ لَا تَقْتُلُوهُ عَسَىٰ أَن يَنفَعَنَا أَوْ نَتَّخِذَهُ وَلَدًا وَهُمْ لَا يَشْعُرُونَ ٩ (28:8-9)

Allah put Musa in these circumstances, and everything that followed his birth was to prepare him for his mission as a prophet. His mission would be to bring a message to the people of Egypt and lead the Israelites out of Egypt.

Interesting fact: Musa's name: The Hebrew form of Musa is "Mosheh." It comes from the word "Mashah," which means to draw out, because he was drawn out of the water. In Coptic "mo" means water and "ushu" means saved.

EXERCISES:

1 Who are the Israelites?

2 Which Surah has a lot of verses about Musa?

3 About how many verses talk about Musa's life in the Quran?

4 Who discovered Musa floating in the chest in the Nile?

5 What caused Musa to have a speech impairment?

6 How was Musa reunited with his mother as a child?

CHAPTER 2

ADULTHOOD

Allah says, And when he reached his maturity, and became established, We gave him wisdom and knowledge. Thus do We reward the virtuous. (28:14)

وَلَمَّا بَلَغَ أَشُدَّهُ وَٱسْتَوَىٰ ءَاتَيْنَٰهُ حُكْمًا وَعِلْمًا وَكَذَٰلِكَ نَجْزِى ٱلْمُحْسِنِينَ (28:14)

As an adult, Musa lived a quiet life, hidden from the public. One day, he heard an Israelite cry out for help, so he rushed to help him.

When he saw the Israelite suffering, his emotions got the best of him, and he unintentionally hit the Egyptian oppressor so hard that he killed him. When this accidental murder became known, it was ordered that Musa be killed in retribution. But he had not intended to kill anyone, he simply did not know his own strength.

Musa realized he had acted excessively and emotionally, and he prayed for Allah's forgiveness.

When he saw the same Israelite in another fight the next day, he realized this man was a trouble maker.

He felt the incident with the Egyptian was a test from Allah. Musa knew he had to learn self-control, and that he would be subjected to Allah's tests and experience Satan's traps and must learn how to act properly.

He asked Allah for forgiveness, and Allah forgave him.

Musa's experiences were important in preparing him for his future message and mission as the deliverer of the Israelites in Egypt and conveyor of the message of Allah's Oneness.

Allah says, Once he entered the city, unnoticed by its people. He found in it two men fighting-one of his own sect, and one from his enemies. The one of his sect solicited his assistance against the one from his enemies; so Musa punched him, and put an end to him. He said, "This is of Satan's doing; he is an enemy that openly misleads."

He said, "My Lord, I have wronged myself, so forgive me." So He forgave him. He is the Forgiver, the Merciful. (28:15-16)

وَدَخَلَ ٱلْمَدِينَةَ عَلَىٰ حِينِ غَفْلَةٍ مِّنْ أَهْلِهَا فَوَجَدَ فِيهَا رَجُلَيْنِ يَقْتَتِلَانِ هَـٰذَا مِن شِيعَتِهِ وَهَـٰذَا مِنْ عَدُوِّهِ فَٱسْتَغَٰثَهُ ٱلَّذِى مِن شِيعَتِهِ عَلَى ٱلَّذِى مِنْ عَدُوِّهِ فَوَكَزَهُۥ مُوسَىٰ فَقَضَىٰ عَلَيْهِ قَالَ هَـٰذَا مِنْ عَمَلِ ٱلشَّيْطَـٰنِ إِنَّهُۥ عَدُوٌّ مُّضِلٌّ مُّبِينٌ ١٥ قَالَ رَبِّ إِنِّى ظَلَمْتُ نَفْسِى فَٱغْفِرْ لِى فَغَفَرَ لَهُۥ إِنَّهُۥ هُوَ ٱلْغَفُورُ ٱلرَّحِيمُ ١٦ (28:15-16)

He said, "My Lord, for the favor You bestowed upon me, I will never be an assistant to the criminals." The next morning, he went about in the city, fearful and vigilant, when the man who had sought his assistance the day before was shouting out to him. Musa said to him, "You are clearly a troublemaker." He said, "My Lord, in as much as you have favored me, I will never be a supporter of the criminals." (28:17-18)

قَالَ رَبِّ بِمَا أَنْعَمْتَ عَلَيَّ فَلَنْ أَكُونَ ظَهِيرًا لِّلْمُجْرِمِينَ ١٧ فَأَصْبَحَ فِى ٱلْمَدِينَةِ خَائِفًا يَتَرَقَّبُ فَإِذَا ٱلَّذِى ٱسْتَنصَرَهُ بِٱلْأَمْسِ يَسْتَصْرِخُهُ ۚ قَالَ لَهُ ۥ مُوسَىٰ إِنَّكَ لَغَوِىٌّ مُّبِينٌ ١٨
(28:17-18)

Allah says, And a man came from the farthest part of the city running. He said, "O Musa, the authorities are considering killing you, so leave; I am giving you good advice." (28:20)

وَجَاءَ رَجُلٌ مِّنْ أَقْصَا ٱلْمَدِينَةِ يَسْعَىٰ قَالَ يَٰمُوسَىٰ إِنَّ ٱلْمَلَأَ يَأْتَمِرُونَ بِكَ لِيَقْتُلُوكَ فَٱخْرُجْ إِنِّى لَكَ مِنَ ٱلنَّٰصِحِينَ (28:20)

Musa left Egypt because there was an order for his capture, and as he traveled, he prayed, 'O my Lord save me from (all) evildoing folk.'

Musa traveled for eight days to a city called Median, between Egypt and Syria. He was now quite far from the Egyptian palace.

When he arrived in Median, he saw a group of people drawing water from a well.

Thirsty from the travels, Musa approached the well, where he found two young women standing patiently and cautiously with their sheep.

Musa sensed the women were in need of help. Forgetting his thirst, he approached them and asked if he could assist them in any way.

Interesting fact: He was surprised that women were shepherding. In that time period, shepherding was considered a man's job.

The older sister said, "We are waiting until the shepherds finish watering their sheep, then we will water ours."

Musa asked, "Why are you waiting?"

The younger one replied, "We cannot push men."

So Musa asked, "Why are you shepherding?"

The younger sister replied, "Our father is an old man, and his health is too poor for him to go outdoors for pasturing sheep."

So Musa offered to water the sheep. Then he asked Allah to bless him with provision. The women asked Musa to accompany them to meet their father, who thanked Musa and invited him to stay with them.

Musa's gentle nature was noticed by the father and his daughters. Musa felt at home with this happy, Allah-conscious, and friendly household.

One of the daughters suggested that her father employ Musa since he was strong and trustworthy. They needed someone like him, especially at the water well, which was often visited by rough people.

The father was pleased with Musa's good character. He approached him and said, "I wish for you to marry one of my daughters on the condition that you agree to work for me for a period of eight years."

Musa agreed. He married the young woman and looked after the old man's herd.

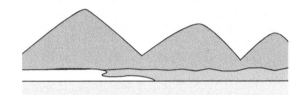

Allah says, As he headed towards Median, he said, "Perhaps my Lord will guide me to the right way." And when he arrived at the waters of Median, he found there a crowd of people drawing water, and he noticed two women waiting on the side. He said, "What is the matter with you?" They said, "We cannot draw water until the shepherds depart, and our father is a very old man." So he drew water for them, and then withdrew to the shade, and said, "My Lord, I am in dire need of whatever good you might send down to me."

Then, one of the two women approached him, walking bashfully. She said, "My father is calling you, to reward you for drawing water for us." And when he came to him, and told him the story, he said, "Do not fear, you have escaped from the wrongdoing people." One of the two women said, "Father, hire him; the best employee for you is the strong and trustworthy."

(28:22-26)

وَلَمَّا تَوَجَّهَ تِلْقَاءَ مَدْيَنَ قَالَ عَسَىٰ رَبِّى أَن يَهْدِيَنِى سَوَآءَ ٱلسَّبِيلِ ٢٢ وَلَمَّا وَرَدَ مَآءَ مَدْيَنَ وَجَدَ عَلَيْهِ أُمَّةً مِّنَ ٱلنَّاسِ يَسْقُونَ وَوَجَدَ مِن دُونِهِمُ ٱمْرَأَتَيْنِ تَذُودَانِّ قَالَ مَا خَطْبُكُمَآ قَالَتَا لَا نَسْقِى حَتَّىٰ يُصْدِرَ ٱلرِّعَآءُ وَأَبُونَا شَيْخٌ كَبِيرٌ ٢٣ فَسَقَىٰ لَهُمَا ثُمَّ تَوَلَّىٰ إِلَى ٱلظِّلِّ فَقَالَ رَبِّ إِنِّى لِمَآ أَنزَلْتَ إِلَىَّ مِنْ خَيْرٍ فَقِيرٌ ٢٤ فَجَآءَتْهُ إِحْدَىٰهُمَا تَمْشِى عَلَى ٱسْتِحْيَآءٍ قَالَتْ إِنَّ أَبِى يَدْعُوكَ لِيَجْزِيَكَ أَجْرَ مَا سَقَيْتَ لَنَآ فَلَمَّا جَآءَهُۥ وَقَصَّ عَلَيْهِ ٱلْقَصَصَ قَالَ لَا تَخَفْ نَجَوْتَ مِنَ ٱلْقَوْمِ ٱلظَّـٰلِمِينَ ٢٥ قَالَتْ إِحْدَىٰهُمَا يَـٰٓأَبَتِ ٱسْتَـْٔجِرْهُ إِنَّ خَيْرَ مَنِ ٱسْتَـْٔجَرْتَ ٱلْقَوِىُّ ٱلْأَمِينُ ٢٦

(28:22-26)

EXERCISES:

1 Did Musa intend to kill the Egyptian oppressor in the fight?

2 What lessons did he learn from this event?

3 What city did Musa escape to?

4 How long did he stay in Median before returning to Egypt?

CHAPTER 3:
REVELATION

The Quran is full of verses about Allah's revelation to Musa. Musa left Median with his family and traveled through the desert until he reached Mount Sinai. There, Musa discovered that he had lost his way.

But Allah showed him the right way. At nightfall they reached Mount Tur. Musa noticed a fire in the distance and said to his family, "I shall fetch a firebrand to warm us."

As he went near the fire, he heard a clear, booming voice calling him, "O Musa, I am Allah, the Lord of the Universe." Musa was confused and looked all around him.

> **Allah says,** When he reached it, he was called from the right side of the valley, at the Blessed Spot, from the bush, "O Musa, it is I, God, the Lord of the Worlds. (28:30)

فَلَمَّا أَتَىٰهَا نُودِىَ مِن شَـٰطِئِ ٱلْوَادِ ٱلْأَيْمَنِ فِى ٱلْبُقْعَةِ ٱلْمُبَـٰرَكَةِ مِنَ ٱلشَّجَرَةِ أَن يَـٰمُوسَىٰٓ إِنِّىٓ أَنَا ٱللَّهُ رَبُّ ٱلْعَـٰلَمِينَ

(28:30)

He again heard the strange voice. The voice said, "And what is in your right hand, O Musa?"

Shivering, he answered, "This is my stick on which I lean, and with which I beat down branches for my sheep with it, and for which I find other uses." This question was asked so that Musa's attention would focus on the stick and to prepare him for the miracle about to happen. This was the beginning of Musa's mission as a prophet.

The same voice commanded him, "Throw down your stick!" He did so, and at once the stick became a wriggling snake. Musa turned to run, but the voice again addressed him, "Fear not and grasp it; We shall return it to its former state." The snake changed back into his stick. Musa's fear was replaced by peace. He realized that he was witnessing the Truth.

Next, Allah commanded him to put his hand into his robe at the armpit. When he pulled it out, the hand had a brilliant shine. Allah then commanded Musa, "You have two signs from your Lord; go to Pharaoh and his chiefs, for they are an evil gang and have crossed all bounds."

Allah says, I am your Lord. Take off your shoes. You are in the sacred valley of Tuwa. I have chosen you, so listen to what is revealed. I am God. There is no God but I. So serve Me, and practice the prayer for My remembrance. (20:12-14)

إِنِّى أَنَا۠ رَبُّكَ فَٱخْلَعْ نَعْلَيْكَ إِنَّكَ بِٱلْوَادِ ٱلْمُقَدَّسِ طُوًى ١٢ وَأَنَا ٱخْتَرْتُكَ فَٱسْتَمِعْ لِمَا يُوحَىٰ ١٣ إِنَّنِى أَنَا ٱللَّهُ لَآ إِلَٰهَ إِلَّآ أَنَا۠ فَٱعْبُدْنِى وَأَقِمِ ٱلصَّلَوٰةَ لِذِكْرِىٓ ١٤ (20:12-14)

The revelation also indicated the specific message of Musa to Pharaoh and the deliverance for the Israelites in Egypt from the tyranny of Pharaoh.

However, Musa feared that he would be arrested by Pharaoh, so he turned to Allah saying, "My Lord! I have killed a man among them and I fear that they will kill me."

Allah says,

(28:33-34)

قَالَ رَبِّ إِنِّى قَتَلْتُ مِنْهُمْ نَفْسًا فَأَخَافُ أَن يَقْتُلُونِ ٣٣ وَأَخِى هَـٰرُونُ هُوَ أَفْصَحُ مِنِّى لِسَانًا فَأَرْسِلْهُ مَعِىَ رِدْءًا يُصَدِّقُنِىٓ إِنِّىٓ أَخَافُ أَن يُكَذِّبُونِ ٣٤

(28:33-34)

"Go, you and your brother, with My signs, and do not neglect My remembrance. Go to Pharaoh. He has tyrannized. But speak to him nicely. Perhaps he will remember, or have some fear." They said, "Lord, we fear he may persecute us, or become violent." He said, "Do not fear. I am with you, I hear and I see. Approach him and say, 'We are the messengers of your Lord, so let the Children of Israel go with us, and do not torment them. We bring you a sign from your Lord, and peace be upon him who follows guidance.

(20:42-47)

ٱذْهَبْ أَنتَ وَأَخُوكَ بِـَٔايَـٰتِى وَلَا تَنِيَا فِى ذِكْرِى ٤٢ ٱذْهَبَآ إِلَىٰ فِرْعَوْنَ إِنَّهُۥ طَغَىٰ ٤٣ فَقُولَا لَهُۥ قَوْلًا لَّيِّنًا لَّعَلَّهُۥ يَتَذَكَّرُ أَوْ يَخْشَىٰ ٤٤ قَالَا رَبَّنَآ إِنَّنَا نَخَافُ أَن يَفْرُطَ عَلَيْنَآ أَوْ أَن يَطْغَىٰ ٤٥ قَالَ لَا تَخَافَآ إِنَّنِى مَعَكُمَآ أَسْمَعُ وَأَرَىٰ ٤٦ فَأْتِيَاهُ فَقُولَآ إِنَّا رَسُولَا رَبِّكَ فَأَرْسِلْ مَعَنَا بَنِىٓ إِسْرَٰٓءِيلَ وَلَا تُعَذِّبْهُمْ قَدْ جِئْنَـٰكَ بِـَٔايَةٍ مِّن رَّبِّكَ وَٱلسَّلَـٰمُ عَلَىٰ مَنِ ٱتَّبَعَ ٱلْهُدَىٰٓ ٤٧

(20:42-47)

Allah granted Musa certain miraculous signs to be presented before Pharaoh as a proof of his truthfulness: turning his stick into a snake and turning his hand to shining white.

Allah says, "Throw down your staff." And when he saw it wiggling, as if it were possessed, he turned his back to flee, and did not look back. "O Musa, come forward, and do not fear, you are perfectly safe. (28:31)

وَأَنْ أَلْقِ عَصَاكَ فَلَمَّا رَءَاهَا تَهْتَزُّ كَأَنَّهَا جَانٌّ وَلَّىٰ مُدْبِرًا وَلَمْ يُعَقِّبْ يَٰمُوسَىٰ أَقْبِلْ وَلَا تَخَفْ إِنَّكَ مِنَ ٱلْءَامِنِينَ (28:31)

Put your hand inside your pocket, and it will come out white, without blemish. And press your arm to your side, against fear. These are two proofs from your Lord, to Pharaoh and his dignitaries. They are truly sinful people." (28:32)

ٱسْلُكْ يَدَكَ فِى جَيْبِكَ تَخْرُجْ بَيْضَاءَ مِنْ غَيْرِ سُوءٍ وَٱضْمُمْ إِلَيْكَ جَنَاحَكَ مِنَ ٱلرَّهْبِ فَذَٰنِكَ بُرْهَٰنَانِ مِن رَّبِّكَ إِلَىٰ فِرْعَوْنَ وَمَلَإِيْهِ إِنَّهُمْ كَانُوا۟ قَوْمًا فَٰسِقِينَ (28:32)

It was natural that Musa, who had known the tyranny of Pharaoh well, feared that Pharaoh might act excessively or tyrannically against him.

And so he prayed to Allah to open his heart, make his task easy, and loosen his speech impairment so that Pharaoh and the leaders around him would understand the message. He also asked Allah to allow his brother Harun to help him in his task.

Allah says, He said, "My Lord, put my heart at peace for me. And ease my task for me. And untie the knot from my tongue. So they can understand my speech. And appoint an assistant for me, from my family. Harun, my brother. Strengthen me with him. And have him share in my mission. That we may glorify You much. And remember You much. You are always watching over us." He said, "You are granted your request, O Musa. We had favored you another time. When We inspired your mother with the inspiration. (20:25-38)

قَالَ رَبِّ ٱشْرَحْ لِى صَدْرِى ٢٥ وَيَسِّرْ لِىَ أَمْرِى ٢٦ وَٱحْلُلْ عُقْدَةً مِّن لِّسَانِى ٢٧ يَفْقَهُواْ قَوْلِى ٢٨ وَٱجْعَل لِّى وَزِيرًا مِّنْ أَهْلِى ٢٩ هَٰرُونَ أَخِى ٣٠ ٱشْدُدْ بِهِۦ أَزْرِى ٣١ وَأَشْرِكْهُ فِىٓ أَمْرِى ٣٢ كَىْ نُسَبِّحَكَ كَثِيرًا ٣٣ وَنَذْكُرَكَ كَثِيرًا ٣٤ إِنَّكَ كُنتَ بِنَا بَصِيرًا ٣٥ قَالَ قَدْ أُوتِيتَ سُؤْلَكَ يَٰمُوسَىٰ ٣٦ وَلَقَدْ مَنَنَّا عَلَيْكَ مَرَّةً أُخْرَىٰٓ ٣٧ إِذْ أَوْحَيْنَآ إِلَىٰٓ أُمِّكَ مَا يُوحَىٰٓ ٣٨

(20:25-38)

Allah accepted his request to have his brother help him. Allah further guided Musa as to how to address the tyrant and deal with him. It was to be a real challenge between a tyrannical oppressor who believed only in himself and the deliverer of the oppressed supported by the All Mighty Allah. Allah also gave Musa comfort by reminding him of all the times in the past during which He had protected Musa.

SIDE BAR. If you look closely at a lot of the Ayahs from the Quran, Allah uses plural pronouns. He is referred to as "We," "Our," or "Us." For example in Ayah 20:23, So that We might make you aware of some of Our greatest wonders. It is a feature of literary style in Arabic that a person may refer to himself or herself by the pronoun 'Nahnu' (we) for respect or glorification. She/he may also use the word 'Ana' (I), indicating one person, or the third person 'Huwa' (he). All three styles are used in the Quran, where Allah addresses the Arabs in their own tongue. In their speech, when there was mention of royalty or glorification, a plural verb conjugation was used. This does not conflict with the concept that Allah is One. It is simply to show power. Normally when the speaker wants to show the magnificence of the act being done or the subject itself, she/he uses plural. The English language has no plural of respect like the Arabic and Hebrew so there is no perfect substitution for those words. Translations just use the word nearest in meaning.

EXERCISES:

1 What made Musa go towards the mountain?

2 What two miracles did Musa witness?

3 What did Musa ask of Allah?

4 Why did Musa want his brother Harun to help him?

CHAPTER 4:
RETURN TO EGYPT

Musa and Harun traveled together to Pharaoh in Egypt and delivered their message. Musa spoke to him about Allah, His mercy, and His Paradise and about the obligations of monotheism and His worship.

Pharaoh listened to Musa's speech with disrespect and aloofness. He thought that Musa was crazy for questioning Pharaoh's supreme position.

After his speech, Pharaoh raised his hand and asked, "What do you want?" Musa answered, "I want you to send the children of Israel with us."

Pharaoh asked, "Why should I send them, when they are my slaves?" Musa replied, "They are the slaves of Allah, Lord of the Worlds." Then Pharaoh asked sarcastically, "Is your name Musa?" Musa said, "Yes."

"Are you not the Musa whom we picked up from the Nile as a helpless baby? Are you not the Musa whom we reared in this palace, who ate and drank from our provisions and who was showered with our wealth? Are you not the Musa who is a fugitive, the killer of an Egyptian man, if my memory does not betray me? It is said that killing is an act of disbelief. Therefore, you were a disbeliever when you killed. You are a fugitive from justice and you come to speak to me! What were you talking about Musa, I forgot?"

Musa knew that Pharaoh was belitting him and threatening him by talking about his past.

Musa ignored his sarcasm and explained that he was not a disbeliever when he killed the Egyptian, he only went astray and Allah the Almighty had not yet given him the revelation at that time. He made Pharaoh understand that he fled from Egypt because he was afraid of their revenge upon him, even though the killing was an accident. He informed him that

Allah had granted
him forgiveness and
made him one of the
messengers.

The Quran describes
their conversation like
this:

Go to Pharaoh, and say, 'We are the Messengers of the Lord of the Worlds. Let the Children of Israel go with us.'"

He said, "Did we not raise you among us as a child, and you stayed among us for many of your years?

And you committed that deed you committed, and you were ungrateful." He said, "I did it then, when I was of those astray. And I fled from you when I feared you; but my Lord gave me wisdom, and made me one of the messengers.

Is that the favor you taunt me with, although you have enslaved the Children of Israel?" Pharaoh said, "And what is the Lord of the Worlds?"

He said, "The Lord of the heavens and the earth, and everything between them, if you are aware." He said to those around him, "Do you not hear?"

He said, "Your Lord and the Lord of your ancestors of old." He said, "This messenger of yours, who is sent to you, is crazy." He said, "Lord of the East and the West, and everything between them, if you understand."

He said, "If you accept any god other than me, I will make you a prisoner."

He said, "What if I bring you something convincing?"

He said, "Bring it, if you are being truthful." (26:16-31)

فَأْتِيَا فِرْعَوْنَ فَقُولَا إِنَّا رَسُولُ رَبِّ ٱلْعَٰلَمِينَ ١٦ أَنْ أَرْسِلْ مَعَنَا بَنِى إِسْرَآءِيلَ ١٧ قَالَ أَلَمْ نُرَبِّكَ فِينَا وَلِيدًا وَلَبِثْتَ فِينَا مِنْ عُمُرِكَ سِنِينَ ١٨ وَفَعَلْتَ فَعْلَتَكَ ٱلَّتِى فَعَلْتَ وَأَنتَ مِنَ ٱلْكَٰفِرِينَ ١٩ قَالَ فَعَلْتُهَا إِذًا وَأَنَا۠ مِنَ ٱلضَّآلِّينَ ٢٠ فَفَرَرْتُ مِنكُمْ لَمَّا خِفْتُكُمْ فَوَهَبَ لِى رَبِّى حُكْمًا وَجَعَلَنِى مِنَ ٱلْمُرْسَلِينَ ٢١ وَتِلْكَ نِعْمَةٌ تَمُنُّهَا عَلَىَّ أَنْ عَبَّدتَّ بَنِى إِسْرَآءِيلَ ٢٢ قَالَ فِرْعَوْنُ وَمَا رَبُّ ٱلْعَٰلَمِينَ ٢٣ قَالَ رَبُّ ٱلسَّمَٰوَٰتِ وَٱلْأَرْضِ وَمَا بَيْنَهُمَآ إِن كُنتُم مُّوقِنِينَ ٢٤ قَالَ لِمَنْ حَوْلَهُۥٓ أَلَا تَسْتَمِعُونَ ٢٥ قَالَ رَبُّكُمْ وَرَبُّ ءَابَآئِكُمُ ٱلْأَوَّلِينَ ٢٦ قَالَ إِنَّ رَسُولَكُمُ ٱلَّذِىٓ أُرْسِلَ إِلَيْكُمْ لَمَجْنُونٌ ٢٧ قَالَ رَبُّ ٱلْمَشْرِقِ وَٱلْمَغْرِبِ وَمَا بَيْنَهُمَآ إِن كُنتُمْ تَعْقِلُونَ ٢٨ قَالَ لَئِنِ ٱتَّخَذْتَ إِلَٰهًا غَيْرِى لَأَجْعَلَنَّكَ مِنَ ٱلْمَسْجُونِينَ ٢٩ قَالَ أَوَلَوْ جِئْتُكَ بِشَىْءٍ مُّبِينٍ ٣٠ قَالَ فَأْتِ بِهِۦٓ إِن كُنتَ مِنَ ٱلصَّٰدِقِينَ ٣١

(26:16-31)

So Musa threw his stick, and it became a serpent. Then he put out his hand, and it was white and glowing. But Pharaoh was not amused. He feared that his rule was in danger so he addressed his advisors, calling Musa and Harun magicians who used illusions. "These are two wizards who will strip you of your best traditions and drive you out of the country with their magic. What do you advise?" he said. The advisors told Pharaoh to imprison Musa and his brother. Then they summoned the best magicians in the country.

He wanted to show everyone that they, too, could do the same magic and change sticks into snakes. He did this in order to decrease the influence that Musa had on the people. He even offered each successful magician a big reward. Pharaoh arranged for a public contest between Musa and the magicians.

All the people were eager and excited to watch this great event. Before it began, Musa stood up and said, "Woe unto you, if you invent a lie against Allah by calling His miracles magic and by not being honest with the Pharaoh. Woe unto you, if you do not know the difference between the truth and falsehood. Allah will destroy you with His punishment, for he who lies against Allah fails miserably."

But the magicians were overruled by their greed for money and glory. They hoped to impress the people with their magic and to expose Musa as a fraud and a cheat.

Musa asked the magicians to perform first. They threw their magical objects down on the ground. Their stick and ropes took the forms of wriggling serpents while the crowd watched in amazement. Pharaoh and his men applauded loudly. Then Musa threw his stick. It began to wriggle and became an enormous snake. The people stood up to see better. Pharaoh and his men sat quietly as, one by one, Musa's huge snake swallowed all the other smaller snakes. Musa bent to pick it up, and it became a stick again in his hand.

The crowd stood up shouting and screaming with excitement. A wonder like this had never been seen before! When the magicians saw this they knew it wasn't magic and bowed to Allah, declaring, "We believe in the Lord of Musa and Harun."

Pharaoh grew very angry and began planning his next move. He accused the magicians and Musa of secretly arranging the stunt. He demanded that the magicians confess to their scheme, threatening them with death.

They refused and stuck to their new belief. No longer hiding his cruel nature, Pharaoh threatened to cut off their hands and feet and to crucify them on the trunks of palm trees as an example to his subjects.

The Quran describes this event:

> We will produce for you magic like it; so make an appointment between us and you, which we will not miss-neither us, nor you-in a central place." He said, "Your appointment is the day of the festival, so let the people be gathered together at mid-morning." Pharaoh turned away, put together his plan, and then came back.
>
> Musa said to them, "Woe to you. Do not fabricate lies against God, or He will destroy you with a punishment. He who invents lies will fail." They disagreed among themselves over their affair, and conferred secretly. They said, "These two are magicians who want to drive you out of your land with their magic, and to abolish your exemplary way of life. So

settle your plan, and come as one front. Today, whoever gains the upper hand will succeed." They said, "O Musa, either you throw, or we will be the first to throw."

He said, "You throw."

And suddenly, their ropes and sticks appeared to him, because of their magic, to be crawling swiftly. So Musa felt apprehensive within himself. We said, "Do not be afraid, you are the uppermost. Now throw down what is in your right hand-it will swallow what they have crafted. What they have crafted is only a magician's trickery.

But the magician will not succeed, no matter what he does." And the magicians fell down prostrate. They said, "We have believed in the Lord of Harun and Musa."

He said, "Did you believe in him before I have given you permission? He must be your chief, who has taught you magic. I will cut off your hands and your feet on alternate sides, and I will crucify you on the trunks of the palm-trees. Then you will know which of us is more severe in punishment, and more lasting."

They said, "We will not prefer you to the proofs that have come to us, and Him who created us. So issue whatever judgment you wish to issue. You can only rule in this lowly life. We have believed in our Lord, so that He may forgive us our sins, and the magic you have compelled us to practice. God is Better, and

Lasting."
Whoever comes to his Lord guilty, for him is Hell, where he neither dies nor lives.
But whoever comes to Him a believer, having worked righteousness- these will have the highest ranks. The Gardens of Perpetuity, beneath which rivers flow, dwelling therein forever. That is the reward for him who purifies himself.
(20:58-76)

Musa and Harun left, and Pharaoh returned to his palace. His emotions changed from amazement and fear to violent rage. He discussed with his ministers, and for no reason commanded them to leave. When he was left alone, he tried to think more calmly. But his anger did not go away.

Then he summoned all the ministers, leaders, and responsible people for a big meeting. Pharaoh entered the meeting with a serious face. It was obvious that he would not surrender easily. He had established a kingdom on the basis of his being a god worshiped by the Egyptian people. Now Musa came to destroy what he had built. Musa said that there was no Lord other than Allah in existence. This meant that Pharaoh was a liar.

Pharaoh opened the meeting by harshly asking Haman (his Prime Minister) a question, "Am I a liar, O Haman?" Haman fell to his knees in amazement and asked, "Who dared to accuse Pharaoh of lying?"

فَلَنَأْتِيَنَّكَ بِسِحْرٍ مِّثْلِهِ فَٱجْعَلْ بَيْنَنَا وَبَيْنَكَ مَوْعِدًا لاَّ نُخْلِفُهُ نَحْنُ وَلاَ أَنتَ مَكَانًا سُوًى ٥٨ قَالَ مَوْعِدُكُمْ يَوْمُ ٱلزِّينَةِ

وَأَن يُحْشَرَ ٱلنَّاسُ ضُحًى ٥٩ فَتَوَلَّىٰ فِرْعَوْنُ فَجَمَعَ كَيْدَهُ ثُمَّ أَتَىٰ ٦٠ قَالَ لَهُم مُّوسَىٰ وَيْلَكُمْ لاَ تَفْتَرُواْ عَلَى ٱللَّهِ

كَذِبًا فَيُسْحِتَكُم بِعَذَابٍ وَقَدْ خَابَ مَنِ ٱفْتَرَىٰ ٦١ فَتَنَازَعُواْ أَمْرَهُم بَيْنَهُمْ وَأَسَرُّواْ ٱلنَّجْوَىٰ ٦٢ قَالُوٓاْ إِنْ هَٰذَانِ

لَسَٰحِرَانِ يُرِيدَانِ أَن يُخْرِجَاكُم مِّنْ أَرْضِكُم بِسِحْرِهِمَا وَيَذْهَبَا بِطَرِيقَتِكُمُ ٱلْمُثْلَىٰ ٦٣ فَأَجْمِعُواْ كَيْدَكُمْ ثُمَّ ٱئْتُواْ صَفًّا

وَقَدْ أَفْلَحَ ٱلْيَوْمَ مَنِ ٱسْتَعْلَىٰ ٦٤ قَالُواْ يَٰمُوسَىٰ إِمَّا أَن تُلْقِىَ وَإِمَّا أَن نَّكُونَ أَوَّلَ مَنْ أَلْقَىٰ ٦٥ قَالَ بَلْ أَلْقُواْ فَإِذَا

حِبَالُهُمْ وَعِصِيُّهُمْ يُخَيَّلُ إِلَيْهِ مِن سِحْرِهِمْ أَنَّهَا تَسْعَىٰ ٦٦ فَأَوْجَسَ فِى نَفْسِهِ خِيفَةً مُّوسَىٰ ٦٧ قُلْنَا لاَ تَخَفْ إِنَّكَ

أَنتَ ٱلْأَعْلَىٰ ٦٨ وَأَلْقِ مَا فِى يَمِينِكَ تَلْقَفْ مَا صَنَعُوٓاْ إِنَّمَا صَنَعُواْ كَيْدُ سَٰحِرٍ وَلاَ يُفْلِحُ ٱلسَّاحِرُ حَيْثُ أَتَىٰ ٦٩ فَأُلْقِىَ

ٱلسَّحَرَةُ سُجَّدًا قَالُوٓاْ ءَامَنَّا بِرَبِّ هَٰرُونَ وَمُوسَىٰ ٧٠ قَالَ ءَامَنتُمْ لَهُ قَبْلَ أَنْ ءَاذَنَ لَكُمْ إِنَّهُ لَكَبِيرُكُمُ ٱلَّذِى عَلَّمَكُمُ

قَالُواْ لَن نُّؤْثِرَكَ عَلَىٰ مَا جَآءَنَا مِنَ ٱلْبَيِّنَٰتِ وَٱلَّذِى فَطَرَنَا فَٱقْضِ مَآ أَنتَ قَاضٍ إِنَّمَا تَقْضِى هَٰذِهِ ٱلْحَيَوٰةَ ٱلدُّنْيَآ ٧٢ إِنَّآ

ءَامَنَّا بِرَبِّنَا لِيَغْفِرَ لَنَا خَطَٰيَٰنَا وَمَآ أَكْرَهْتَنَا عَلَيْهِ مِنَ ٱلسِّحْرِ وَٱللَّهُ خَيْرٌ وَأَبْقَىٰ ٧٣ إِنَّهُ مَن يَأْتِ رَبَّهُ مُجْرِمًا فَإِنَّ لَهُ

جَهَنَّمَ لاَ يَمُوتُ فِيهَا وَلاَ يَحْيَىٰ ٧٤ وَمَن يَأْتِهِ مُؤْمِنًا قَدْ عَمِلَ ٱلصَّٰلِحَٰتِ فَأُوْلَٰئِكَ لَهُمُ ٱلدَّرَجَٰتُ ٱلْعُلَىٰ ٧٥ جَنَّٰتُ عَدْنٍ

تَجْرِى مِن تَحْتِهَا ٱلْأَنْهَٰرُ خَٰلِدِينَ فِيهَا وَذَٰلِكَ جَزَآءُ مَن تَزَكَّىٰ ٧٦

(20:58-76)

Pharaoh said, "Has Musa not said that there is a Lord in Heaven?" Haman answered, "Musa is lying." Turning his face to the other side, Pharaoh said, "I know he is a liar." Then he looked towards Haman and said, "O Haman! Build me a tower so that I may arrive at the heavens, and I may look upon the god of Musa but verily, I still think he is a liar."

> The Quran says, And Pharaoh said, O Haman! Build for me a tower that haply I may reach the roads. The pathways of the heavens, so that I may glance at the God of Musa; though I think he is lying." Thus Pharaoh's evil deeds were made to appear good to him, and he was averted from the path. Pharaoh's guile was only in defeat.
> (40:36-37)

Pharaoh proclaimed his royal command to build a lofty tower, its height to reach the heavens. He ignored the rules of engineering. But in spite of this, Haman agreed, knowing that it was impossible to build such a tower. He said that he would issue a command to build it immediately.

"However, your majesty, let me object to Pharaoh for the first time. You will never find anyone in the heavens. There is no god but you." At the end of the meeting, Pharaoh said, "O chiefs! I know no god other than me."

Pharaoh held many meetings after that one. He summoned the army, the police, the director of intelligence, the ministers, princes, and priests. Pharaoh asked his director of intelligence, "What do people say?"

He said, "My men have spread a rumor among them that Musa won the contest against the magicians because of a plot and that a major magician had joined with him in this plan. The plot had been disclosed, and we believe an

وَقَالَ فِرْعَوْنُ يَـٰهَـٰمَنُ ٱبْنِ لِى صَرْحًا لَّعَلِّى أَبْلُغُ ٱلْأَسْبَـٰبَ ٣٦ أَسْبَـٰبَ ٱلسَّمَـٰوَٰتِ فَأَطَّلِعَ إِلَىٰ إِلَـٰهِ مُوسَىٰ وَإِنِّى لَأَظُنُّهُۥ كَـٰذِبًا ۚ وَكَذَٰلِكَ زُيِّنَ لِفِرْعَوْنَ سُوٓءُ عَمَلِهِۦ وَصُدَّ عَنِ ٱلسَّبِيلِ وَمَا كَيْدُ فِرْعَوْنَ إِلَّا فِى تَبَابٍ ٣٧

(40:36-37)

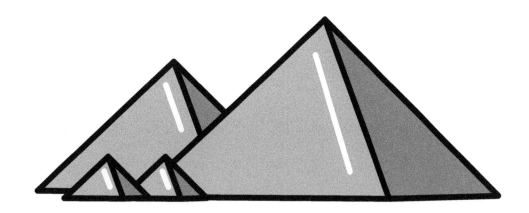

unknown authority financed it."

Pharaoh asked his director of police, "What about the magicians' corpses?" He said, "My men hung them in public squares and markets to terrify the people. We will spread a rumor that Pharaoh will kill whoever had anything to do with the plot." Pharaoh and his people made examples of those they killed in order to spread fear among the people in the hopes of keeping them away from Musa's message.

Then Pharaoh asked the commander of the army, "What does the army say?" He said, "The army hopes that commands will be issued to move in whatever direction Pharaoh desires."

Pharaoh said, "The role of the army has not come yet. Its role will come." Pharaoh fell silent. Haman, the Prime Minister, moved and raised his hand to speak. Pharaoh allowed him to speak and Haman asked, "Will we leave Musa and his people to corrupt the rest of the people on the earth so that they leave your worship?"

Pharaoh said, "You read my thoughts, O Haman." He issued commands, and Pharaoh's men rushed to terrorize and oppress whomever objected to these acts.

Musa stood watching what was happening. He did not have the power to stop these acts. All he could do was to tell his people to be patient and have faith in God's promise. He ordered them to ask Allah the Almighty for a catastrophe on the Egyptians.

EXERCISES:

1 What does aloof mean?

2 What was the punishment for those who disobeyed Pharaoh and didn't believe in his divinity?

3 What happened after Musa turned his stick into a snake?

4 Describe the events of the magic show.

The Israelites were suffering badly from Pharaoh's acts. They complained to Musa:

> They said, "We were persecuted before you came to us, and after you came to us." He said, "Perhaps your Lord will destroy your enemy, and make you successors in the land; then He will see how you behave." (7:129)

قَالُوٓاْ أُوذِينَا مِن قَبْلِ أَن تَأْتِيَنَا وَمِنۢ بَعْدِ مَا جِئْتَنَا قَالَ عَسَىٰ رَبُّكُمْ أَن يُهْلِكَ عَدُوَّكُمْ وَيَسْتَخْلِفَكُمْ فِى ٱلْأَرْضِ فَيَنظُرَ كَيْفَ تَعْمَلُونَ (7:129)

Musa was facing a difficult situation. He had to confront Pharaoh and stop his tyranny. Pharaoh believed that Musa was threatening his kingdom and ordered that Musa be killed. However a vote proved that killing him would not be a good idea. Musa only said that Allah is his Lord. There were two possibilities; either Musa was righteous or a liar. If he lied, he would be responsible for his lie. If he was righteous and they slayed him, where was the guarantee that they would be rescued from the torment of Allah? Either way, he neither said nor did anything that merited his killing.

This angered Pharaoh and his counselors and they threatened to hurt the man that voted against his killing, but the man did not change his opinion.

The Quran describes this situation, Pharaoh said, "Leave me to kill Musa, and let him appeal to his Lord. I fear he may change your religion, or spread disorder in the land." Musa said, "I have sought the protection of my Lord and your Lord, from every tyrant who does not believe in the Day of Account." A believing man from Pharaoh's family, who had concealed his faith, said, "Are you going to kill a man for saying, `My Lord is God,' and he has brought you clear proofs from your Lord? If he is a liar, his lying will rebound upon him; but if he is truthful, then some of what he promises you will befall you. God does not guide the extravagant impostor. O my people! Yours is the dominion today, supreme in the land; but who will help us against God's might, should it fall upon us?"

Pharaoh said, "I do not show you except what I see, and I do not guide you except to the path of prudence. The one who had believed said, "O my people, I fear for you the like of the day of the confederates. Like the fate of the people of Nooh, and Aad, and Thamood, and those after them. God wants no injustice for the servants.

O my people, I fear for you the Day of Calling Out. The Day when you will turn and flee, having no defender against God. Whomever God misguides has no guide." Joseph had come to you with clear revelations, but you continued to doubt what he came to you with.

Until, when he perished, you said, "God will never send a messenger after him." Thus God leads astray the outrageous skeptic. Those who argue against God's revelations, without any proof having come to them-a heinous sin in the sight of God, and of those who believe. Thus God seals the heart of every proud bully.

And Pharaoh said, "O Hamaan, build me a tower, that I may reach the pathways. The pathways of the heavens, so that I may glance at the God of Musa; though I think he is lying." Thus Pharaoh's evil deeds were made to appear good to him, and he was averted from the path. Pharaoh's guile was only in defeat.

The one who had believed said, "O my people, follow me, and I will guide you to the path of rectitude." "O my people, the life of this world is nothing but fleeting enjoyment, but the Hereafter is the Home of Permanence. Whoever commits a sin will be repaid only with its like.

But whoever works righteousness, whether male or female, and is a believer-these will enter Paradise, where they will be provided for without account. O my people, how is it that I call you to salvation, and you call me to the Fire? You call me to reject God, and to associate with Him what I have no knowledge of, while I call you to the Mighty Forgiver.

Without a doubt, what you call me to has no say in this world, or in the Hereafter; and our turning back is to God; and the transgressors are the inmates of the Fire. You will remember what I am telling you, so I commit my case to God. God is Observant of the servants." So God protected him from the evils of their scheming, while a terrible torment besieged Pharaoh's clan. (40:26-45)

وَقَالَ فِرْعَوْنُ ذَرُونِى أَقْتُلْ مُوسَىٰ وَلْيَدْعُ رَبَّهُ ۖ إِنِّى أَخَافُ أَن يُبَدِّلَ دِينَكُمْ أَوْ أَن يُظْهِرَ فِى ٱلْأَرْضِ ٱلْفَسَادَ ٢٦ وَقَالَ مُوسَىٰ إِنِّى عُذْتُ بِرَبِّى وَرَبِّكُم مِّن كُلِّ مُتَكَبِّرٍ لَّا يُؤْمِنُ بِيَوْمِ ٱلْحِسَابِ ٢٧ وَقَالَ رَجُلٌ مُّؤْمِنٌ مِّنْ ءَالِ فِرْعَوْنَ يَكْتُمُ إِيمَٰنَهُ أَتَقْتُلُونَ رَجُلًا أَن يَقُولَ رَبِّىَ ٱللَّهُ وَقَدْ جَاءَكُم بِٱلْبَيِّنَٰتِ مِن رَّبِّكُمْ ۖ وَإِن يَكُ كَٰذِبًا فَعَلَيْهِ كَذِبُهُۥ ۖ وَإِن يَكُ صَادِقًا يُصِبْكُم بَعْضُ ٱلَّذِى يَعِدُكُمْ ۖ إِنَّ ٱللَّهَ لَا يَهْدِى مَنْ هُوَ مُسْرِفٌ كَذَّابٌ ٢٨ يَٰقَوْمِ لَكُمُ ٱلْمُلْكُ ٱلْيَوْمَ ظَٰهِرِينَ فِى ٱلْأَرْضِ فَمَن يَنصُرُنَا مِنۢ بَأْسِ ٱللَّهِ إِن جَاءَنَا ۚ قَالَ فِرْعَوْنُ مَا أُرِيكُمْ إِلَّا مَا أَرَىٰ وَمَا أَهْدِيكُمْ إِلَّا سَبِيلَ ٱلرَّشَادِ ٢٩ وَقَالَ ٱلَّذِىٓ ءَامَنَ يَٰقَوْمِ إِنِّىٓ أَخَافُ عَلَيْكُم مِّثْلَ يَوْمِ ٱلْأَحْزَابِ ٣٠ مِثْلَ دَأْبِ قَوْمِ نُوحٍ وَعَادٍ وَثَمُودَ وَٱلَّذِينَ مِنۢ بَعْدِهِمْ ۚ وَمَا ٱللَّهُ يُرِيدُ ظُلْمًا لِّلْعِبَادِ ٣١ وَيَٰقَوْمِ إِنِّىٓ أَخَافُ عَلَيْكُمْ يَوْمَ ٱلتَّنَادِ ٣٢ يَوْمَ تُوَلُّونَ مُدْبِرِينَ مَا لَكُم مِّنَ ٱللَّهِ مِنْ عَاصِمٍ وَمَن يُضْلِلِ ٱللَّهُ فَمَا لَهُۥ مِنْ هَادٍ ٣٣ وَلَقَدْ جَاءَكُمْ يُوسُفُ مِن قَبْلُ بِٱلْبَيِّنَٰتِ فَمَا زِلْتُمْ فِى شَكٍّ مِّمَّا جَاءَكُم بِهِۦ ۖ حَتَّىٰٓ إِذَا هَلَكَ قُلْتُمْ لَن يَبْعَثَ ٱللَّهُ مِنۢ بَعْدِهِۦ رَسُولًا ۚ كَذَٰلِكَ يُضِلُّ ٱللَّهُ مَنْ هُوَ مُسْرِفٌ مُّرْتَابٌ ٣٤ ٱلَّذِينَ يُجَٰدِلُونَ فِىٓ ءَايَٰتِ ٱللَّهِ بِغَيْرِ سُلْطَٰنٍ أَتَىٰهُمْ ۖ كَبُرَ مَقْتًا عِندَ ٱللَّهِ وَعِندَ ٱلَّذِينَ ءَامَنُوا۟ ۚ كَذَٰلِكَ يَطْبَعُ ٱللَّهُ عَلَىٰ كُلِّ قَلْبِ مُتَكَبِّرٍ جَبَّارٍ ٣٥ وَقَالَ فِرْعَوْنُ يَٰهَٰمَٰنُ ٱبْنِ لِى صَرْحًا لَّعَلِّىٓ أَبْلُغُ ٱلْأَسْبَٰبَ ٣٦ أَسْبَٰبَ ٱلسَّمَٰوَٰتِ فَأَطَّلِعَ إِلَىٰٓ إِلَٰهِ مُوسَىٰ وَإِنِّى لَأَظُنُّهُۥ كَٰذِبًا ۚ وَكَذَٰلِكَ زُيِّنَ لِفِرْعَوْنَ سُوٓءُ عَمَلِهِۦ وَصُدَّ عَنِ ٱلسَّبِيلِ ۚ وَمَا كَيْدُ فِرْعَوْنَ إِلَّا فِى تَبَابٍ ٣٧ وَقَالَ ٱلَّذِىٓ ءَامَنَ يَٰقَوْمِ ٱتَّبِعُونِ أَهْدِكُمْ سَبِيلَ ٱلرَّشَادِ ٣٨ يَٰقَوْمِ إِنَّمَا هَٰذِهِ ٱلْحَيَوٰةُ ٱلدُّنْيَا مَتَٰعٌ وَإِنَّ ٱلْءَاخِرَةَ هِىَ دَارُ ٱلْقَرَارِ ٣٩ مَنْ عَمِلَ سَيِّئَةً فَلَا يُجْزَىٰٓ إِلَّا مِثْلَهَا ۖ وَمَنْ عَمِلَ صَٰلِحًا مِّن ذَكَرٍ أَوْ أُنثَىٰ وَهُوَ مُؤْمِنٌ فَأُو۟لَٰٓئِكَ يَدْخُلُونَ ٱلْجَنَّةَ يُرْزَقُونَ فِيهَا بِغَيْرِ حِسَابٍ ٤٠ ۞ وَيَٰقَوْمِ مَا لِىٓ أَدْعُوكُمْ إِلَى ٱلنَّجَوٰةِ وَتَدْعُونَنِىٓ إِلَى ٱلنَّارِ ٤١ تَدْعُونَنِى لِأَكْفُرَ بِٱللَّهِ وَأُشْرِكَ بِهِۦ مَا لَيْسَ لِى بِهِۦ عِلْمٌ وَأَنَا۠ أَدْعُوكُمْ إِلَى ٱلْعَزِيزِ ٱلْغَفَّٰرِ ٤٢ لَا جَرَمَ أَنَّمَا تَدْعُونَنِىٓ إِلَيْهِ لَيْسَ لَهُۥ دَعْوَةٌ فِى ٱلدُّنْيَا وَلَا فِى ٱلْءَاخِرَةِ وَأَنَّ مَرَدَّنَآ إِلَى ٱللَّهِ وَأَنَّ ٱلْمُسْرِفِينَ هُمْ أَصْحَٰبُ ٱلنَّارِ ٤٣ فَسَتَذْكُرُونَ مَآ أَقُولُ لَكُمْ ۚ وَأُفَوِّضُ أَمْرِىٓ إِلَى ٱللَّهِ ۚ إِنَّ ٱللَّهَ بَصِيرٌ بِٱلْعِبَادِ ٤٤ فَوَقَىٰهُ ٱللَّهُ سَيِّئَاتِ مَا مَكَرُوا۟ ۖ وَحَاقَ بِـَٔالِ فِرْعَوْنَ سُوٓءُ ٱلْعَذَابِ ٤٥

(40:26-45)

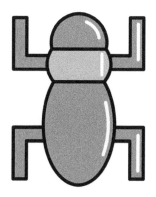

Musa approached Pharaoh again. He repeated his demand that he free the slaves of Israel. In response, Pharaoh called all the people of Egypt to a huge gathering where he reminded them that he was their lord who provided for them and that Musa was just a poor man.

They were limited in their knowledge and only believed what they saw in front of them, so many of them believed Pharaoh's words and started ignoring Musa.

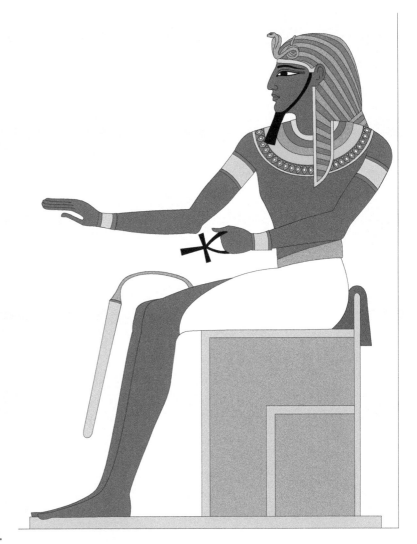

After that, Allah commanded Musa to warn Pharaoh of a harsh punishment in this world. As a warning to Pharaoh, Allah created a drought in Egypt. The Nile did not flood its banks to soak the dry land as it normally did. And because of that the crops did not grow, which led to starvation. But even after that, Pharaoh stayed arrogant. So Allah caused a huge flood, which destroyed the land.

Interesting fact: The children of Israel were very easily influenced. Because they were oppressed for a very long time, they were not very knowledgeable and often lacked insight or vision.

After the drought and the flood, the Egyptians asked Musa to pray to his Lord and remove the punishment.

Musa prayed to Allah, and Allah removed the suffering caused by the flood. The waters returned to normal and the crops began to grow again. But when Musa went to them to fulfill their promise to release the children of Israel, they did not respond. So Allah sent more punishments on them. After the drought and the flood, Allah sent thousands of locusts into Pharaoh's land which ate all the crops that they had grown. Once again Pharaoh's people asked Musa to remove the punishment and promised to release the Children of Israel in return. But after the locusts left, they did not fulfill their promise again. Then Allah sent another plague. He spread disease-carrying lice amongst the Egyptians. Once again, Pharaoh's people asked Musa to remove the punishment and promised to release the Children of Israel.

Suddenly, the land filled with frogs. They jumped on their food, went into their houses, and caused so much irritation that the people were scared to open their mouths for fear of a frog jumping into it. Once again, Pharaoh's people asked Musa to remove the punishment and promised to release the Children of Israel. But after the frogs left, they did not fulfill their promise.

Then Allah changed the Nile water into blood. When Musa and his people drank the water it was ordinary water. However, if any Egyptian filled a cup with the water, it became blood. Once again Pharaoh's people asked Musa to remove the punishment and promised to release the Children of Israel. But after the blood left they did not fulfill their promise.

The Quran says, And We afflicted the people of Pharaoh with barren years, and with shortage of crops, that they may take heed. When something good came their way, they said, "This is ours." And when something bad happened to them, they ascribed the evil omen to Musa and those with him. In fact, their omen is with God, but most of them do not know.

And they said, "No matter what sign you bring us, to bewitch us with, we will not believe in you. "So We let loose upon them the flood, and the locusts, and the lice, and the frogs, and blood-all explicit signs-but they were too arrogant. They were a sinful people. Whenever a plague befell them, they would say, "O Musa, pray to your Lord for us, according to the covenant He made with you. If you lift the plague from us, we will believe in you, and let the Children of Israel go with you."

But when We lifted the plague from them, for a term they were to fulfill, they broke their promise.
(7:130-135)

Pharaoh became ruder and more arrogant than before any of these five punishments. "Pharaoh is the only god. Has he not the kingdom of Egypt and rivers flowing under it?" Pharaoh asked his people. He declared that Musa was a liar, a magician, and a poor man who did not wear even one bracelet of gold.

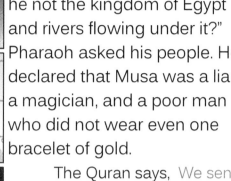

The Quran says, We sent Musa with Our revelations to Pharaoh and his dignitaries. He said, "I am the Messenger of the Lord of the Worlds."

But when he showed them Our signs, they started laughing at them. Each sign We showed them was more

وَلَقَدْ أَخَذْنَآ ءَالَ فِرْعَوْنَ بِٱلسِّنِينَ وَنَقْصٍ مِّنَ ٱلثَّمَرَٰتِ لَعَلَّهُمْ يَذَّكَّرُونَ ١٣٠ فَإِذَا جَآءَتْهُمُ ٱلْحَسَنَةُ قَالُوا۟ لَنَا هَٰذِهِۦ ۖ وَإِن تُصِبْهُمْ سَيِّئَةٌ يَطَّيَّرُوا۟ بِمُوسَىٰ وَمَن مَّعَهُۥٓ ۗ أَلَآ إِنَّمَا طَٰٓئِرُهُمْ عِندَ ٱللَّهِ وَلَٰكِنَّ أَكْثَرَهُمْ لَا يَعْلَمُونَ ١٣١ وَقَالُوا۟ مَهْمَا تَأْتِنَا بِهِۦ مِنْ ءَايَةٍ لِّتَسْحَرَنَا بِهَا فَمَا نَحْنُ لَكَ بِمُؤْمِنِينَ ١٣٢ فَأَرْسَلْنَا عَلَيْهِمُ ٱلطُّوفَانَ وَٱلْجَرَادَ وَٱلْقُمَّلَ وَٱلضَّفَادِعَ وَٱلدَّمَ ءَايَٰتٍ مُّفَصَّلَٰتٍ فَٱسْتَكْبَرُوا۟ وَكَانُوا۟ قَوْمًا مُّجْرِمِينَ ١٣٣ وَلَمَّا وَقَعَ عَلَيْهِمُ ٱلرِّجْزُ قَالُوا۟ يَٰمُوسَى ٱدْعُ لَنَا رَبَّكَ بِمَا عَهِدَ عِندَكَ ۖ لَئِن كَشَفْتَ عَنَّا ٱلرِّجْزَ لَنُؤْمِنَنَّ لَكَ وَلَنُرْسِلَنَّ مَعَكَ بَنِىٓ إِسْرَٰٓءِيلَ ١٣٤ فَلَمَّا كَشَفْنَا عَنْهُمُ ٱلرِّجْزَ إِلَىٰٓ أَجَلٍ هُم بَٰلِغُوهُ إِذَا هُمْ يَنكُثُونَ ١٣٥

(7:130-135)

marvelous than its counterpart. And We afflicted them with the plagues, so that they may repent.

They said, "O sorcerer, pray to your Lord for us, according to His pledge to you, and then we will be guided."

But when We lifted the torment from them, they immediately broke their promise. Pharaoh proclaimed among his people, saying, "O my people, do I not own the Kingdom of Egypt, and these rivers flow beneath me? Do you not see?

Am I not better than this miserable wretch, who can barely express himself? Why are bracelets of gold not dropped on him, or they angels came with him in procession?"

So he fooled his people, and they obeyed him. They were wicked people. And when they provoked Our wrath, We took retribution from them, and We drowned them all. Thus We made them a precedent and an example for the others. (43:46-56)

Musa had to inspire his people to keep believing.

وَلَقَدْ أَرْسَلْنَا مُوسَىٰ بِـَٔايَٰتِنَا إِلَىٰ فِرْعَوْنَ وَمَلَإِيْهِۦ فَقَالَ إِنِّى رَسُولُ رَبِّ ٱلْعَٰلَمِينَ ٤٦ فَلَمَّا جَآءَهُم بِـَٔايَٰتِنَا إِذَا هُم مِّنْهَا يَضْحَكُونَ ٤٧ وَمَا نُرِيهِم مِّنْ ءَايَةٍ إِلَّا هِىَ أَكْبَرُ مِنْ أُخْتِهَا وَأَخَذْنَٰهُم بِٱلْعَذَابِ لَعَلَّهُمْ يَرْجِعُونَ ٤٨ وَقَالُوا۟ يَٰٓأَيُّهَ ٱلسَّاحِرُ ٱدْعُ لَنَا رَبَّكَ بِمَا عَهِدَ عِندَكَ إِنَّنَا لَمُهْتَدُونَ ٤٩ فَلَمَّا كَشَفْنَا عَنْهُمُ ٱلْعَذَابَ إِذَا هُمْ يَنكُثُونَ ٥٠ وَنَادَىٰ فِرْعَوْنُ فِى قَوْمِهِۦ قَالَ يَٰقَوْمِ أَلَيْسَ لِى مُلْكُ مِصْرَ وَهَٰذِهِ ٱلْأَنْهَٰرُ تَجْرِى مِن تَحْتِىٓ أَفَلَا تُبْصِرُونَ ٥١ أَمْ أَنَا۠ خَيْرٌ مِّنْ هَٰذَا ٱلَّذِى هُوَ مَهِينٌ وَلَا يَكَادُ يُبِينُ ٥٢ فَلَوْلَآ أُلْقِىَ عَلَيْهِ أَسْوِرَةٌ مِّن ذَهَبٍ أَوْ جَآءَ مَعَهُ ٱلْمَلَٰٓئِكَةُ مُقْتَرِنِينَ ٥٣ فَٱسْتَخَفَّ قَوْمَهُۥ فَأَطَاعُوهُ إِنَّهُمْ كَانُوا۟ قَوْمًا فَٰسِقِينَ ٥٤ فَلَمَّآ ءَاسَفُونَا ٱنتَقَمْنَا مِنْهُمْ فَأَغْرَقْنَٰهُمْ أَجْمَعِينَ ٥٥ فَجَعَلْنَٰهُمْ سَلَفًا وَمَثَلًا لِّلْءَاخِرِينَ ٥٦

(43:46-56)

The Quran says, But none believed in Musa except some children of his people, for fear that Pharaoh and his chiefs would persecute them. Pharaoh was high and mighty in the land. He was a tyrant.

Musa said, "O my people, if you have believed in God, then put your trust in Him, if you have submitted." They said, "In God we have put our trust. Our Lord, do not make us victims of the oppressive people."

"And deliver us, by Your mercy, from the disbelieving people." (10:83-86)

It was obvious that Pharaoh was never going to be convinced of Musa's message and he would not stop the torture of the Children of Israel. So, Musa prayed to Allah, "Our Lord! You have bestowed on Pharaoh and his chiefs splendor and wealth in the life of this world, our Lord! That they may lead men astray from Your Path. Our Lord! Destroy their wealth, and harden their hearts, so that they will not believe until they see the painful torment."

فَمَآ ءَامَنَ لِمُوسَىٰٓ إِلَّا ذُرِّيَّةٌ مِّن قَوْمِهِۦ عَلَىٰ خَوْفٍ مِّن فِرْعَوْنَ وَمَلَإِيْهِمْ أَن يَفْتِنَهُمْ وَإِنَّ فِرْعَوْنَ لَعَالٍ فِى ٱلْأَرْضِ وَإِنَّهُۥ لَمِنَ ٱلْمُسْرِفِينَ ٨٣ وَقَالَ مُوسَىٰ يَٰقَوْمِ إِن كُنتُمْ ءَامَنتُم بِٱللَّهِ فَعَلَيْهِ تَوَكَّلُوٓا۟ إِن كُنتُم مُّسْلِمِينَ ٨٤ فَقَالُوا۟ عَلَى ٱللَّهِ تَوَكَّلْنَا رَبَّنَا لَا تَجْعَلْنَا فِتْنَةً لِّلْقَوْمِ ٱلظَّٰلِمِينَ ٨٥ وَنَجِّنَا بِرَحْمَتِكَ مِنَ ٱلْقَوْمِ ٱلْكَٰفِرِينَ ٨٦

(10:83-86)

1   List the punishments that Allah sent on Pharaoh and his people.

2   What are locusts? Look one up on the internet and draw one.

3   What does "breach" mean?

4   How many times did Pharaoh promise to release the Children of Israel but breach his promise?

Pharaoh had five chances to believe in Allah and release the Children of Israel from slavery and persecution. But he did not change and instead ordered to have Musa killed. So Allah put an end to his crimes and told Musa to depart from Egypt in the darkness of night.

Musa led his people out of Egypt towards the Red Sea. By morning they reached an impassable beach. By then Pharaoh became aware of their departure, so he sent a large army to go after them. The Israelites became impatient and Joshua (Yusha), Ibn Nun, said, "In front of us is this impassable barrier, the sea, and behind us the enemy; this will surely be the end for us!"

Musa responded to him by saying that they must wait for guidance from Allah. This gave them some hope. Allah then instructed Musa to strike the sea with his stick. Musa did that and a strong wind blew over the beach. The sun was very bright. Then, miraculously, the sea started to split in half with the waves standing high on each side.

The people followed Musa through the split. This miracle proved that Allah was with them. Following not too far behind them, they saw Pharaoh and his army approaching.

The people panicked and Musa instructed them to hurry across. Pharaoh and his army rushed to cross the parted waters but when they were midway Allah commanded the sea to return to its former state and the waters collapsed drowning him and his entire army.

Allah says in the Quran, And We inspired Musa, saying, "Take away My slaves by night, verily, you will be pursued." Then Pharaoh sent callers to all the cities. Saying, "Verily! These indeed are but a small band. And verily, they have done what enrages us; We are ready, assembled, and forewarned."

> The Quran says, So, We expelled them from gardens and springs, treasures, and every kind of honorable place. Thus (We turned them Pharaoh's people) out, and We caused the children of Israel to inherit them. So they pursued them at sunrise. And when the two hosts saw each other, the people of Musa said, "We are sure to be overtaken."

He said, "No; my Lord is with me, He will guide me." We inspired Musa, "Strike the sea with your staff." Whereupon it parted, and each part was like a huge hill. And there We brought the others near. And We saved Musa and those with him, all together. Then We drowned the others. In that there is a sign, but most of them are not believers. Surely, your Lord is the Almighty, the Merciful. (26:57-68)

فَأَخْرَجْنَٰهُم مِّن جَنَّٰتٍ وَعُيُونٍ ٥٧ وَكُنُوزٍ وَمَقَامٍ كَرِيمٍ ٥٨ كَذَٰلِكَ وَأَوْرَثْنَٰهَا بَنِىٓ إِسْرَٰٓءِيلَ ٥٩ فَأَتْبَعُوهُم مُّشْرِقِينَ ٦٠ فَلَمَّا تَرَٰٓءَا ٱلْجَمْعَانِ قَالَ أَصْحَٰبُ مُوسَىٰٓ إِنَّا لَمُدْرَكُونَ ٦١ قَالَ كَلَّآ إِنَّ مَعِىَ رَبِّى سَيَهْدِينِ ٦٢ فَأَوْحَيْنَآ إِلَىٰ مُوسَىٰٓ أَنِ ٱضْرِب بِّعَصَاكَ ٱلْبَحْرَ فَٱنفَلَقَ فَكَانَ كُلُّ فِرْقٍ كَٱلطَّوْدِ ٱلْعَظِيمِ ٦٣ وَأَزْلَفْنَا ثَمَّ ٱلْأَخَرِينَ ٦٤ وَأَنجَيْنَا مُوسَىٰ وَمَن مَّعَهُۥٓ أَجْمَعِينَ ٦٥ ثُمَّ أَغْرَقْنَا ٱلْأَخَرِينَ ٦٦ إِنَّ فِى ذَٰلِكَ لَءَايَةً وَمَا كَانَ أَكْثَرُهُم مُّؤْمِنِينَ ٦٧ وَإِنَّ رَبَّكَ لَهُوَ ٱلْعَزِيزُ ٱلرَّحِيمُ ٦٨

(26:57-68)

In another Surah, the Quran says, And We delivered the Children of Israel across the sea. Pharaoh and his troops pursued them, defiantly and aggressively. Until, when he was about to drown, he said, "I believe that there is no god except the One the Children of Israel believe in, and I am of those who submit."

Now? When you have rebelled before, and been of the mischief-makers? Today We will preserve your body, so that you become a sign for those after you. But most people are heedless of Our signs. (10:90-92)

وَجَٰوَزْنَا بِبَنِىٓ إِسْرَٰٓءِيلَ ٱلْبَحْرَ فَأَتْبَعَهُمْ فِرْعَوْنُ وَجُنُودُهُۥ بَغْيًا وَعَدْوًا حَتَّىٰٓ إِذَآ أَدْرَكَهُ ٱلْغَرَقُ قَالَ ءَامَنتُ أَنَّهُۥ لَآ إِلَٰهَ إِلَّا ٱلَّذِىٓ ءَامَنَتْ بِهِۦ بَنُوٓا۟ إِسْرَٰٓءِيلَ وَأَنَا۠ مِنَ ٱلْمُسْلِمِينَ ٩٠ ءَآلْـَٰٔنَ وَقَدْ عَصَيْتَ قَبْلُ وَكُنتَ مِنَ ٱلْمُفْسِدِينَ ٩١ فَٱلْيَوْمَ نُنَجِّيكَ بِبَدَنِكَ لِتَكُونَ لِمَنْ خَلْفَكَ ءَايَةً وَإِنَّ كَثِيرًا مِّنَ ٱلنَّاسِ عَنْ ءَايَٰتِنَا لَغَٰفِلُونَ ٩٢

(10:90-92)

Pharaoh died but his influence on the Israelites did not. Their years of oppression had a great effect on them. Their attitudes towards submission to one God were ruined. They had tortured souls. Many of them were ignorant and stubborn.

This attitude and state of mind came out in everything they did. And it began to make things difficult on Musa's leadership.

But for now, they were still in amazement at the miracle of the parting of the sea. The miracle of the parting of the sea was so powerful that even Pharaoh declared his belief in Allah just before drowning. The Israelites had strong hearts but their belief strengthened and weakened throughout time. For example, on their journey through the desert, when they passed by a group of people worshipping idols they turned to Musa and asked him to specify a god for them to worship as those other people did. They were jealous of the other people and their idols.

The Quran says, And We delivered the Children of Israel across the sea. And when they came upon a people who were devoted to some statues of theirs, they said, "O Musa, make for us a god, as they have gods." He said, "You are truly an ignorant people."

"What these people are concerned with is perdition, and their deeds are based on falsehoods." He said, "Shall I seek for you a god other than God, when He has favored you over all other people?"

Remember how We saved you from Pharaoh's people, who subjected you to the worst of sufferings-killing your sons and sparing your women. In that was a tremendous trial from your Lord. (7:138-141)

وَجَٰوَزْنَا بِبَنِىٓ إِسْرَٰٓءِيلَ ٱلْبَحْرَ فَأَتَوْا۟ عَلَىٰ قَوْمٍ يَعْكُفُونَ عَلَىٰٓ أَصْنَامٍ لَّهُمْ قَالُوا۟ يَٰمُوسَى ٱجْعَل لَّنَآ إِلَٰهًا كَمَا لَهُمْ ءَالِهَةٌ قَالَ إِنَّكُمْ قَوْمٌ تَجْهَلُونَ ١٣٨ إِنَّ هَٰٓؤُلَآءِ مُتَبَّرٌ مَّا هُمْ فِيهِ وَبَٰطِلٌ مَّا كَانُوا۟ يَعْمَلُونَ ١٣٩ قَالَ أَغَيْرَ ٱللَّهِ أَبْغِيكُمْ إِلَٰهًا وَهُوَ فَضَّلَكُمْ عَلَى ٱلْعَٰلَمِينَ ١٤٠ وَإِذْ أَنجَيْنَٰكُم مِّنْ ءَالِ فِرْعَوْنَ يَسُومُونَكُمْ سُوٓءَ ٱلْعَذَابِ يُقَتِّلُونَ أَبْنَآءَكُمْ وَيَسْتَحْيُونَ نِسَآءَكُمْ وَفِى ذَٰلِكُم بَلَآءٌ مِّن رَّبِّكُمْ عَظِيمٌ ١٤١

(7:138-141)

Allah favored the Israelites by saving them from Pharaoh's oppression and giving them water in the dryness of the desert when they were thirsty. When they needed water, Allah commanded Musa to strike a rock, which made twelve springs of water for the twelve different tribes. Allah also kept the skies cloudy to protect them from the burning sun.

Interesting fact: To feed the Israelites while on exodus, Allah

1   At what point did the Israelites lose some hope on their exodus?

2   What happened when Musa's army reached the beach?

3   In your own words explain why the Israelites had "tortured souls."

CHAPTER 7:
LIVING & ROAMING IN

Among the Israelites were some bad spirited people. They confused people and made them unappreciative for how they were living. Some people became disgusted with the food; they asked for onions, garlic, beans, and lentils, which were the traditional Egyptian foods. They asked Musa to pray to Allah for these foods. Musa was mad at them and pointed out to them that they needed to appreciate what they were given instead of wanting to return to oppression in Egypt.

> The Quran says, And recall when Musa prayed for water for his people. We said, "Strike the rock with your staff." Thereupon twelve springs gushed out from it, and each tribe recognized its drinking-place. "Eat and drink from God's provision, and do not corrupt the earth with disobedience."
>
> And recall when you said, "O Musa, we cannot endure one kind of food, so call to your Lord to produce for us of what the earth grows: of its herbs, and its cucumbers, and its garlic, and its lentils, and its onions." He said, "Would you substitute worse for better? Go down to Egypt, where you will have what you asked for." They were struck with humiliation and poverty, and incurred wrath from God. That was because they rejected God's revelations and wrongfully killed the prophets. That was because they disobeyed and transgressed.
> (2:60-61)

وَإِذِ ٱسْتَسْقَىٰ مُوسَىٰ لِقَوْمِهِۦ فَقُلْنَا ٱضْرِب بِّعَصَاكَ ٱلْحَجَرَ فَٱنفَجَرَتْ مِنْهُ ٱثْنَتَا عَشْرَةَ عَيْنًا قَدْ عَلِمَ كُلُّ أُنَاسٍ مَّشْرَبَهُمْ كُلُواْ وَٱشْرَبُواْ مِن رِّزْقِ ٱللَّهِ وَلَا تَعْثَوْاْ فِى ٱلْأَرْضِ مُفْسِدِينَ ٦٠ وَإِذْ قُلْتُمْ يَٰمُوسَىٰ لَن نَّصْبِرَ عَلَىٰ طَعَامٍ وَٰحِدٍ فَٱدْعُ لَنَا رَبَّكَ يُخْرِجْ لَنَا مِمَّا تُنۢبِتُ ٱلْأَرْضُ مِنۢ بَقْلِهَا وَقِثَّآئِهَا وَفُومِهَا وَعَدَسِهَا وَبَصَلِهَا قَالَ أَتَسْتَبْدِلُونَ ٱلَّذِى هُوَ أَدْنَىٰ بِٱلَّذِى هُوَ خَيْرٌ ٱهْبِطُواْ مِصْرًا فَإِنَّ لَكُم مَّا سَأَلْتُمْ وَضُرِبَتْ عَلَيْهِمُ ٱلذِّلَّةُ وَٱلْمَسْكَنَةُ وَبَآءُو بِغَضَبٍ مِّنَ ٱللَّهِ ذَٰلِكَ بِأَنَّهُمْ كَانُواْ يَكْفُرُونَ بِـَٔايَٰتِ ٱللَّهِ وَيَقْتُلُونَ ٱلنَّبِيِّـۧنَ بِغَيْرِ ٱلْحَقِّ ذَٰلِكَ بِمَا عَصَواْ وَّكَانُواْ يَعْتَدُونَ ٦١ (2:60-61)

Allah had told Musa to lead the Israelites to the Promised Land (Palestine). Palestine was promised to Prophet Ibrahim. It is a land for Allah-conscious people. But the Children of Israel said, "O Musa! In this Holy Land are strong, intimidating people, and we shall never enter it, till they leave it; when they leave, then we will enter."

HE DESERT

In response to the Israelites' fear of the strong people in the holy land, two God-fearing men said, "Confront them at the gate, for when you are in, victory will be yours, and put your trust in Allah if you are believers indeed." They responded, "O Musa! We will never enter it as long as they are there. So go you, and your Lord and fight you two. We are sitting right here." Musa turned to Allah when met by their complaning and said, "O my Lord! I have power only over myself and my brother, so separate us from the people who are the rebellious and disobedient to Allah!" After all Allah granted them, they kept returning to bad behavior. Only a handful of people were willing to fight alongside Musa.

It seemed that many of the Israelites feared everything and were not prepared to make any sacrifices. Even though Pharaoh was dead, his effect on them still remained. They needed a very long recovery. Musa even prayed to Allah saying that he wished to not be judged alongside these people and to be able to differentiate between the good and bad among them. It seemed that the nature of this generation of people was corrupted. It was decreed that they must roam the desert. A new generation was necessary for success.

The Quran says, When Musa said to his people, "O my people, remember God's blessings upon you, when He placed prophets among you, and made you kings, and gave you what He never gave any other people." "O my people, enter the Holy Land which God has assigned for you, and do not turn back, lest you return as losers." They said, "O Musa, there are tyrannical people in it; we will not enter it until they leave it. If they leave it, we will be entering." Two men of those who feared, but whom God had blessed, said, "Go at them by the gate; and when you have entered it, you will prevail. And put your trust in God, if you are believers." They said, "O Musa, we will not enter it, ever, as long as they are in it. So go ahead, you and your Lord, and fight. We are staying right here." (5:20-26)

وَإِذْ قَالَ مُوسَىٰ لِقَوْمِهِ يَٰقَوْمِ ٱذْكُرُوا۟ نِعْمَةَ ٱللَّهِ عَلَيْكُمْ إِذْ جَعَلَ فِيكُمْ أَنۢبِيَآءَ وَجَعَلَكُم مُّلُوكًا وَءَاتَىٰكُم مَّا لَمْ يُؤْتِ أَحَدًا مِّنَ ٱلْعَٰلَمِينَ ٢٠ يَٰقَوْمِ ٱدْخُلُوا۟ ٱلْأَرْضَ ٱلْمُقَدَّسَةَ ٱلَّتِى كَتَبَ ٱللَّهُ لَكُمْ وَلَا تَرْتَدُّوا۟ عَلَىٰٓ أَدْبَارِكُمْ فَتَنقَلِبُوا۟ خَٰسِرِينَ ٢١ قَالُوا۟ يَٰمُوسَىٰٓ إِنَّ فِيهَا قَوْمًا جَبَّارِينَ وَإِنَّا لَن نَّدْخُلَهَا حَتَّىٰ يَخْرُجُوا۟ مِنْهَا فَإِن يَخْرُجُوا۟ مِنْهَا فَإِنَّا دَٰخِلُونَ ٢٢ قَالَ رَجُلَانِ مِنَ ٱلَّذِينَ يَخَافُونَ أَنْعَمَ ٱللَّهُ عَلَيْهِمَا ٱدْخُلُوا۟ عَلَيْهِمُ ٱلْبَابَ فَإِذَا دَخَلْتُمُوهُ فَإِنَّكُمْ غَٰلِبُونَ وَعَلَى ٱللَّهِ فَتَوَكَّلُوٓا۟ إِن كُنتُم مُّؤْمِنِينَ ٢٣ قَالُوا۟ يَٰمُوسَىٰٓ إِنَّا لَن نَّدْخُلَهَآ أَبَدًا مَّا دَامُوا۟ فِيهَا فَٱذْهَبْ أَنتَ وَرَبُّكَ فَقَٰتِلَآ إِنَّا هَٰهُنَا قَٰعِدُونَ ٢٤ قَالَ رَبِّ إِنِّى لَآ أَمْلِكُ إِلَّا نَفْسِى وَأَخِى فَٱفْرُقْ بَيْنَنَا وَبَيْنَ ٱلْقَوْمِ ٱلْفَٰسِقِينَ ٢٥ قَالَ فَإِنَّهَا مُحَرَّمَةٌ عَلَيْهِمْ أَرْبَعِينَ سَنَةً يَتِيهُونَ فِى ٱلْأَرْضِ فَلَا تَأْسَ عَلَى ٱلْقَوْمِ ٱلْفَٰسِقِينَ ٢٦ (5:20-26)

The Israelites roamed the land aimlessly for about forty years. During that time they entered Sinai. Musa came to the same place where he had spoken to Allah for the first time. He went to Allah for guidance in ruling over his people. Allah told him to purify himself by fasting for thirty days. After that he was to go to Mount Sinai to receive the laws that would govern his people.

The Quran says, And We appointed to Musa thirty nights, and completed them with ten; and thus the time appointed by his Lord was forty nights. And Musa said to his brother Harun, "Take my place among my people, and be upright, and do not follow the way of the mischief-makers." And when Musa came to Our appointment, and his Lord spoke to him, he said, "My Lord, allow me to look and see You." He said, "You will not see Me, but look at the mountain; if it stays in its place, you will see Me." But when his Lord manifested Himself to the mountain, He turned it into dust, and Musa fell down unconscious. Then, when he recovered, he said, "Glory be to you, I repent to you, and I am the first of the believers."

He said, "O Musa, I have chosen you over all people for My messages and for My Words. So take what I have given you, and be one of the thankful." And We inscribed for him in the Tablets all kinds of enlightenments, and decisive explanation of all things. "Hold fast to them, and exhort your people to adopt the best of them. I will show you the fate of the sinners." (7:142-145)

وَوَاعَدْنَا مُوسَىٰ ثَلَٰثِينَ لَيْلَةً وَأَتْمَمْنَٰهَا بِعَشْرٍ فَتَمَّ مِيقَٰتُ رَبِّهِۦٓ أَرْبَعِينَ لَيْلَةً وَقَالَ مُوسَىٰ لِأَخِيهِ هَٰرُونَ ٱخْلُفْنِى فِى قَوْمِى وَأَصْلِحْ وَلَا تَتَّبِعْ سَبِيلَ ٱلْمُفْسِدِينَ ١٤٢ وَلَمَّا جَآءَ مُوسَىٰ لِمِيقَٰتِنَا وَكَلَّمَهُۥ رَبُّهُۥ قَالَ رَبِّ أَرِنِىٓ أَنظُرْ إِلَيْكَ قَالَ لَن تَرَىٰنِى وَلَٰكِنِ ٱنظُرْ إِلَى ٱلْجَبَلِ فَإِنِ ٱسْتَقَرَّ مَكَانَهُۥ فَسَوْفَ تَرَىٰنِى فَلَمَّا تَجَلَّىٰ رَبُّهُۥ لِلْجَبَلِ جَعَلَهُۥ دَكًّا وَخَرَّ مُوسَىٰ صَعِقًا فَلَمَّآ أَفَاقَ قَالَ سُبْحَٰنَكَ تُبْتُ إِلَيْكَ وَأَنَا۠ أَوَّلُ ٱلْمُؤْمِنِينَ ١٤٣ قَالَ يَٰمُوسَىٰٓ إِنِّى ٱصْطَفَيْتُكَ عَلَى ٱلنَّاسِ بِرِسَٰلَٰتِى وَبِكَلَٰمِى فَخُذْ مَآ ءَاتَيْتُكَ وَكُن مِّنَ ٱلشَّٰكِرِينَ ١٤٤ وَكَتَبْنَا لَهُۥ فِى ٱلْأَلْوَاحِ مِن كُلِّ شَىْءٍ مَّوْعِظَةً وَتَفْصِيلًا لِّكُلِّ شَىْءٍ فَخُذْهَا بِقُوَّةٍ وَأْمُرْ قَوْمَكَ يَأْخُذُوا۟ بِأَحْسَنِهَا سَأُو۟رِيكُمْ دَارَ ٱلْفَٰسِقِينَ ١٤٥

(7:142-145)

I will turn away from My revelations those who behave proudly on earth without justification. Even if they see every sign, they will not believe in it; and if they see the path of rectitude, they will not adopt it for a path; and if they see the path of error, they will adopt it for a path. That is because they denied Our revelations, and paid no attention to them.

Those who deny Our revelations and the meeting of the Hereafter-their deeds will come to nothing. Will they be repaid except according to what they used to do? (7:146-147)

سَأَصْرِفُ عَنْ ءَايَـٰتِىَ ٱلَّذِينَ يَتَكَبَّرُونَ فِى ٱلْأَرْضِ بِغَيْرِ ٱلْحَقِّ وَإِن يَرَوْا۟ كُلَّ ءَايَةٍ لَّا يُؤْمِنُوا۟ بِهَا وَإِن يَرَوْا۟ سَبِيلَ ٱلرُّشْدِ لَا يَتَّخِذُوهُ سَبِيلًا وَإِن يَرَوْا۟ سَبِيلَ ٱلْغَىِّ يَتَّخِذُوهُ سَبِيلًا ذَٰلِكَ بِأَنَّهُمْ كَذَّبُوا۟ بِـَٔايَـٰتِنَا وَكَانُوا۟ عَنْهَا غَـٰفِلِينَ ١٤٦ وَٱلَّذِينَ كَذَّبُوا۟ بِـَٔايَـٰتِنَا وَلِقَآءِ ٱلْءَاخِرَةِ حَبِطَتْ أَعْمَـٰلُهُمْ هَلْ يُجْزَوْنَ إِلَّا مَا كَانُوا۟ يَعْمَلُونَ ١٤٧ (7:146-147)

Musa's commandments in the Quran: Say, "Come, let me tell you what your Lord has forbidden you: that you associate nothing with Him; that you honor your parents; that you do not kill your children because of poverty-We provide for you and for them; that you do not come near indecencies, whether outward or inward; and that you do not kill the soul which God has sanctified-except in the course of justice. All this He has enjoined upon you, so that you may understand." And do not come near the property of the orphan, except with the best intentions, until he reaches maturity. And give full weight and full measure, equitably. We do not burden any soul beyond its capacity. And when you speak, be fair, even if it concerns a close relative. And fulfill your covenant with God. All this He has enjoined upon you, so that you may take heed. (6:151-152)

قُل تَعَالَوْا۟ أَتْلُ مَا حَرَّمَ رَبُّكُمْ عَلَيْكُمْ أَلَّا تُشْرِكُوا۟ بِهِۦ شَيْـًٔا وَبِٱلْوَٰلِدَيْنِ إِحْسَـٰنًا وَلَا تَقْتُلُوٓا۟ أَوْلَـٰدَكُم مِّنْ إِمْلَـٰقٍ نَّحْنُ نَرْزُقُكُمْ وَإِيَّاهُمْ وَلَا تَقْرَبُوا۟ ٱلْفَوَٰحِشَ مَا ظَهَرَ مِنْهَا وَمَا بَطَنَ وَلَا تَقْتُلُوا۟ ٱلنَّفْسَ ٱلَّتِى حَرَّمَ ٱللَّهُ إِلَّا بِٱلْحَقِّ ذَٰلِكُمْ وَصَّىٰكُم بِهِۦ لَعَلَّكُمْ تَعْقِلُونَ ١٥١ وَلَا تَقْرَبُوا۟ مَالَ ٱلْيَتِيمِ إِلَّا بِٱلَّتِى هِىَ أَحْسَنُ حَتَّىٰ يَبْلُغَ أَشُدَّهُۥ وَأَوْفُوا۟ ٱلْكَيْلَ وَٱلْمِيزَانَ بِٱلْقِسْطِ لَا نُكَلِّفُ نَفْسًا إِلَّا وُسْعَهَا وَإِذَا قُلْتُمْ فَٱعْدِلُوا۟ وَلَوْ كَانَ ذَا قُرْبَىٰ وَبِعَهْدِ ٱللَّهِ أَوْفُوا۟ ذَٰلِكُمْ وَصَّىٰكُم بِهِۦ لَعَلَّكُمْ تَذَكَّرُونَ ١٥٢ (6:151-152)

EXERCISES:

1 Did the Israelites cooperate with Musa or give him a hard time?

2 Where did they go during the forty years of roaming?

3 What happened when Musa went to seek help from Allah?

4 What are the Commandments to Musa's people from Allah?

CHAPTER 8:

THE CALF

Musa had been gone on the mountain receiving the commandments for forty days. His people lived at they bottom of the mountain and they were starting to become restless. A man among the people decided to take matters in his own hands. This man, Samiri, said to the people that they must find another god for guidance. He offered to make one for them out of gold jewelry. So he dug a big hole and told everyone to put their gold and jewelry into it. Many people blindly followed his orders. Then he set it on fire to melt down the metals.

He even acted as a magician by making hand gestures. From the melted metal he made a golden calf. The calf was made to be hollow and when the wind passed through it, it made a loud sound. The people thought this was magical and must be from a real god. So some of them accepted the golden calf as their god. Harun, Musa's brother, who acted as their leader while Musa was gone was extremely disappointed. He said to the people, "O my people! You have been deceived. Your Lord is the Most Beneficent. Follow and obey me." They replied, "We will stop worshiping this god only if Musa returns." There were some, however, who remained believers and they separated themselves from the ones who went against the moral code.

When Musa came down from the mountain, he saw people singing and dancing around this golden calf. He was very mad. He threw down the tablet that contained the ten commandments. He went to Harun and pulled on his beard saying, "What held you back when you saw them going astray? Why did you not fight this corruption?"

Harun replied, "O son of my mother, let go of my beard!" Harun composed himself and explained that stopping them from worshiping the calf would have been difficult and divided the group. He said, "The group considered me weak and were about to kill me. So don't make the enemies rejoice over me, nor put me among the people who are wrong-doers."

Musa understood Harun's helplessness. After his anger subsided and he was feeling better, Musa began to deal with the situation.

And the people of Musa made in his absence, out of their ornaments, the image of a calf (for worship). It had a sound (as if it was mooing). Did they not see that it could neither speak to them nor guide them to the way? They took it (for worship) and they were wrong-doers. (7:148)

وَاتَّخَذَ قَوْمُ مُوسَىٰ مِنْ بَعْدِهِ مِنْ حُلِيِّهِمْ عِجْلاً جَسَدًا لَّهُ خُوَارٌ أَلَمْ يَرَوْاْ أَنَّهُ لَا يُكَلِّمُهُمْ وَلَا يَهْدِيهِمْ سَبِيلاً اتَّخَذُوهُ وَكَانُواْ ظَلِمِينَ ١٤٨ (7:148)

[Allah] said, "And what made you hasten from your people, O Moses?" He said, "They are close upon my tracks, and I hastened to You, my Lord, that You be pleased." [Allah] said, "But indeed, We have tried your people after you [departed], and the Samiri has led them astray." So Moses returned to his people, angry and grieved. He said, "O my people, did your Lord not make you a good promise? Then, was the time [of its fulfillment] too long for you, or did you wish that wrath from your Lord descend upon you, so you broke your promise [of obedience] to me?" They said, "We did not break our promise to you by our will, but we were made to carry burdens from the ornaments of the people [of Pharaoh], so we threw them [into the fire], and thus did the Samiri throw." TAnd he extracted for them [the statue of] a calf which had a lowing sound, and they said, "This is your god and the god of Moses, but he forgot." Did they not see that it could not return to them any speech and that it did not possess for them any harm or benefit? And Aaron had already told them before [the return of Moses], "O my people, you are only being tested by it, and indeed, your Lord is the Most Merciful, so follow me and obey my order." They said, "We will never cease being devoted to the calf until Moses returns to us."

(20:83-91)

وَمَا أَعْجَلَكَ عَن قَوْمِكَ يَمُوسَىٰ ٨٣ قَالَ هُمْ أُوْلَاءِ عَلَىٰ أَثَرِى وَعَجِلْتُ إِلَيْكَ رَبِّ لِتَرْضَىٰ ٨٤ قَالَ فَإِنَّا قَدْ فَتَنَّا قَوْمَكَ مِن بَعْدِكَ وَأَضَلَّهُمُ ٱلسَّامِرِىُّ ٨٥ فَرَجَعَ مُوسَىٰ إِلَىٰ قَوْمِهِ غَضْبَٰنَ أَسِفًا قَالَ يَٰقَوْمِ أَلَمْ يَعِدْكُمْ رَبُّكُمْ وَعْدًا حَسَنًا أَفَطَالَ عَلَيْكُمُ ٱلْعَهْدُ أَمْ أَرَدتُّمْ أَن يَحِلَّ عَلَيْكُمْ غَضَبٌ مِّن رَّبِّكُمْ فَأَخْلَفْتُم مَّوْعِدِى ٨٦ قَالُواْ مَا أَخْلَفْنَا مَوْعِدَكَ بِمَلْكِنَا وَلَٰكِنَّا حُمِّلْنَا أَوْزَارًا مِّن زِينَةِ ٱلْقَوْمِ فَقَذَفْنَٰهَا فَكَذَٰلِكَ أَلْقَى ٱلسَّامِرِىُّ ٨٧ فَأَخْرَجَ لَهُمْ عِجْلًا جَسَدًا لَّهُ خُوَارٌ فَقَالُواْ هَٰذَا إِلَٰهُكُمْ وَإِلَٰهُ مُوسَىٰ فَنَسِىَ ٨٨ أَفَلَا يَرَوْنَ أَلَّا يَرْجِعُ إِلَيْهِمْ قَوْلًا وَلَا يَمْلِكُ لَهُمْ ضَرًّا وَلَا نَفْعًا ٨٩ وَلَقَدْ قَالَ لَهُمْ هَٰرُونُ مِن قَبْلُ يَٰقَوْمِ إِنَّمَا فُتِنتُم بِهِ وَإِنَّ رَبَّكُمُ ٱلرَّحْمَٰنُ فَٱتَّبِعُونِى وَأَطِيعُواْ أَمْرِى ٩٠ قَالُواْ لَن نَّبْرَحَ عَلَيْهِ عَٰكِفِينَ حَتَّىٰ يَرْجِعَ إِلَيْنَا مُوسَىٰ ٩١

(20:83-91)

The Quran speaks more about what happened when Musa returned. He said, "O Harun, what prevented you, when you saw them going astray. From following me? Did you disobey my command?" He said, "Son of my mother, do not seize me by my beard or my head. I feared you would say, `You have caused division among the Children of Israel, and did not regard my word.'"

He said, "What do you have to say, O Samarian?"

He said, "I saw what they did not see, so I grasped a handful from the Messenger's traces, and I flung it away. Thus my soul prompted me."

He said, "Begone! Your lot in this life is to say, 'No contact.' And you have an appointment that you will not miss. Now look at your god that you remained devoted to-we will burn it up, and then blow it away into the sea, as powder." (20:92-97)

قَالَ يَهَٰرُونُ مَا مَنَعَكَ إِذْ رَأَيْتَهُمْ ضَلُّوٓاْ ٩٢ أَلَّا تَتَّبِعَنِّ أَفَعَصَيْتَ أَمْرِى ٩٣ قَالَ يَبْنَؤُمَّ لَا تَأْخُذْ بِلِحْيَتِى وَلَا بِرَأْسِىٓ إِنِّى خَشِيتُ أَن تَقُولَ فَرَّقْتَ بَيْنَ بَنِىٓ إِسْرَٰٓءِيلَ وَلَمْ تَرْقُبْ قَوْلِى ٩٤ قَالَ فَمَا خَطْبُكَ يَٰسَٰمِرِىُّ ٩٥ قَالَ بَصُرْتُ بِمَا لَمْ يَبْصُرُواْ بِهِۦ فَقَبَضْتُ قَبْضَةً مِّنْ أَثَرِ ٱلرَّسُولِ فَنَبَذْتُهَا وَكَذَٰلِكَ سَوَّلَتْ لِى نَفْسِى ٩٦ قَالَ فَٱذْهَبْ فَإِنَّ لَكَ فِى ٱلْحَيَوٰةِ أَن تَقُولَ لَا مِسَاسَ وَإِنَّ لَكَ مَوْعِدًا لَّن تُخْلَفَهُۥ وَٱنظُرْ إِلَىٰٓ إِلَٰهِكَ ٱلَّذِى ظَلْتَ عَلَيْهِ عَاكِفًا لَّنُحَرِّقَنَّهُۥ ثُمَّ لَنَنسِفَنَّهُۥ فِى ٱلْيَمِّ نَسْفًا ٩٧
(20:92-97)

However, the punishment which was imposed upon the calf worshippers was severe.

The Quran says, And remember when Musa said to his people, "O my people! Verily, you have wronged yourselves by worshipping the calf. So turn in repentance to your Creator and kill yourselves (the innocent kill the wrongdoers among you), that will be better for you with your Creator." Then He accepted your repentance. Truly, He is the One Who accepts repentance, the Most Merciful. And remember when you said, "O Musa, We shall never believe in you till we see Allah plainly." But you were seized with a thunderbolt (lightning) while you were looking. Then We raised you up after your death, so that you might be grateful.
(2:54-56)

وَإِذْ قَالَ مُوسَىٰ لِقَوْمِهِۦ يَٰقَوْمِ إِنَّكُمْ ظَلَمْتُمْ أَنفُسَكُم بِٱتِّخَاذِكُمُ ٱلْعِجْلَ فَتُوبُوٓاْ إِلَىٰ بَارِئِكُمْ فَٱقْتُلُوٓاْ أَنفُسَكُمْ ذَٰلِكُمْ خَيْرٌ لَّكُمْ عِندَ بَارِئِكُمْ فَتَابَ عَلَيْكُمْ إِنَّهُۥ هُوَ ٱلتَّوَّابُ ٱلرَّحِيمُ ٥٤ وَإِذْ قُلْتُمْ يَٰمُوسَىٰ لَن نُّؤْمِنَ لَكَ حَتَّىٰ نَرَى ٱللَّهَ جَهْرَةً فَأَخَذَتْكُمُ ٱلصَّٰعِقَةُ وَأَنتُمْ تَنظُرُونَ ٥٥ ثُمَّ بَعَثْنَٰكُم مِّنۢ بَعْدِ مَوْتِكُمْ لَعَلَّكُمْ تَشْكُرُونَ ٥٦
(2:54-56)

Their crime did not go unpunished. Musa told them to repent, to ask for forgiveness from Allah. Musa then returned to Mount Sinai with seventy elders and there he spoke with Allah. Allah spoke to Musa directly, but the rest saw it happen. This should have been a great miracle to witness, however, it was not enough to make them believe. They said to Musa, "O Musa! We shall never believe in you until we see Allah plainly."

This proved once and for all that these people had hard hearts. Their comment about wanting to see Allah to be convinced, after witnessing miracle after miracle, was punished with lightning and earth quaking. All their bodies fell dead. But Musa's tender heart made him appeal to Allah telling Him that they are ignorant, foolish people who do not know any better. So Allah forgave them.

The Quran says, And Musa chose from his people seventy men for Our appointment. When the tremor shook them, he said, "My Lord, had You willed, You could have destroyed them before, and me too. Will you destroy us for what the fools among us have done? This is but Your test-with it You misguide whomever You will, and guide whomever You will. You are our Protector, so forgive us, and have mercy on us. You are the Best of Forgivers."

"And inscribe for us goodness in this world, and in the Hereafter. We have turned to You." He said, "My punishment is inflicted upon whomever I will, but My mercy encompasses all things. I will specify it for those who act righteously and practice regular charity, and those who believe in Our signs."

Those who follow the Messenger, the Unlettered Prophet, whom they find mentioned in the Torah and the Gospel in their possession. He directs them to righteousness, and deters them from evil, and allows for them all good things, and prohibits for them wickedness, and unloads the burdens and the shackles that are upon them. Those who believe in him, and respect him, and support him, and follow the light that came down with him-these are the successful. (7:155-157)

وَٱخْتَارَ مُوسَىٰ قَوْمَهُ سَبْعِينَ رَجُلاً لِّمِيقَٰتِنَا فَلَمَّا أَخَذَتْهُمُ ٱلرَّجْفَةُ قَالَ رَبِّ لَوْ شِئْتَ أَهْلَكْتَهُم مِّن قَبْلُ وَإِيَّٰىَ أَتُهْلِكُنَا بِمَا فَعَلَ ٱلسُّفَهَاءُ مِنَّا إِنْ هِيَ إِلاَّ فِتْنَتُكَ تُضِلُّ بِهَا مَن تَشَاءُ وَتَهْدِى مَن تَشَاءُ أَنتَ وَلِيُّنَا فَٱغْفِرْ لَنَا وَٱرْحَمْنَا وَأَنتَ خَيْرُ ٱلْغَٰفِرِينَ ١٥٥ وَٱكْتُبْ لَنَا فِى هَٰذِهِ ٱلدُّنْيَا حَسَنَةً وَفِى ٱلْآخِرَةِ إِنَّا هُدْنَا إِلَيْكَ قَالَ عَذَابِىَ أُصِيبُ بِهِ مَنْ أَشَاءُ وَرَحْمَتِى وَسِعَتْ كُلَّ شَىْءٍ فَسَأَكْتُبُهَا لِلَّذِينَ يَتَّقُونَ وَيُؤْتُونَ ٱلزَّكَوٰةَ وَٱلَّذِينَ هُم بِآيَٰتِنَا يُؤْمِنُونَ ١٥٦ ٱلَّذِينَ يَتَّبِعُونَ ٱلرَّسُولَ ٱلنَّبِىَّ ٱلْأُمِّىَّ ٱلَّذِى يَجِدُونَهُ مَكْتُوبًا عِندَهُمْ فِى ٱلتَّوْرَٰةِ وَٱلإِنجِيلِ يَأْمُرُهُم بِٱلْمَعْرُوفِ وَيَنْهَٰهُمْ عَنِ ٱلْمُنكَرِ وَيُحِلُّ لَهُمُ ٱلطَّيِّبَٰتِ وَيُحَرِّمُ عَلَيْهِمُ ٱلْخَبَٰئِثَ وَيَضَعُ عَنْهُمْ إِصْرَهُمْ وَٱلأَغْلَٰلَ ٱلَّتِى كَانَتْ عَلَيْهِمْ فَٱلَّذِينَ ءَامَنُوا بِهِ وَعَزَّرُوهُ وَنَصَرُوهُ وَٱتَّبَعُوا ٱلنُّورَ ٱلَّذِى أُنزِلَ مَعَهُ أُوْلَٰئِكَ هُمُ ٱلْمُفْلِحُونَ ١٥٧

(7:155-157)

EXERCISES:

1   What did Musa see when he returned from the mountain?

2   What does "repent" mean?

3   Why did Harun not stop the calf worshippers while Musa was gone?

CHAPTER 9:

MUSA & THE PEOPLE

The story of the boy and the cow:

There was a family made up of a father, mother, and small son. The father was a very good, righteous man. He did everything for the sake of Allah and was honest in everything he did.

When he was dying his last words were, "O Allah, I place my wife, my little son, and my only possession, a calf, in Your care." But then he asked his wife to take the calf into the forest and let it go. He did this because he did not trust the selfish and greedy children of Israel to care for it for his wife and child.

After a few years, when the boy had grown up, his mother told him, "Your father has left you a calf in the trust of Allah. It must have grown into a cow by now." The son was surprised. He did not know about the calf all these years and asked his mother where it was. She replied, "Be like your father and say: 'I trust in Allah, then go look for it.'"

So he took a rope and went to the forest. He bowed to Allah and said, "O Allah, Lord of Abraham and Jacob and Job, return to me my father's trust." As he raised his head, he saw the cow coming towards him. It walked up to him then stopped right beside him. He tied the rope around its neck and led it to his house. The cow became very close to the boy and wouldn't let anyone else milk him.

The boy lived an honest life just like his father did. He worked as a wood cutter. He even divided all his earnings in thirds. One third he gave to his mother, kept one third for himself, and donated one third to charity. His nights, too, were divided into three parts: during the evenings he helped his mother, then later he prayed, and during the last part he rested.

Around the same time, in the same village, a man was killed by some evil people who wanted his wealth.

So his other relatives went to Musa and asked him for help to try to find these evil murderers. Musa gave them instructions in order to find them: 1. Go slaughter a cow; 2. Remove its tongue; and 3. Put it on the dead body.

The relatives did not believe in this method and mocked Musa for his suggestion. He told them, "Allah forbid that I be foolish!" So they asked him many many questions about his plan. They asked him about the type of cow they should slaughter, and he said, "This cow should be neither young nor mature, but in between the two conditions, so do as you have been commanded." Instead of following his direction, they asked him more questions. "What color must it be?" He replied, "Verily, it should be yellow in color."

They still were not satisfied with his answer and asked for more details. With each question came more requirements. Musa replied, "It is a cow not trained to till the earth or water the fields: a perfect and unblemished cow." So they went out to look for a cow with this description. The only one that matched the description was the one owned by the boy. They met him and asked to buy the cow. He told them he would have to ask his mother first, so they went with him to his house and offered her three gold coins. She did not accept their offer, saying that the cow was worth much more.

They kept offering more and more but she kept refusing. Finally they asked the son to persuade his mother to be reasonable. He told them, "I will not sell the cow without my mother's approval, even if you offered me its skin filled with gold!" On hearing this, his mother smiled and said, "Let that be the price: its skin filled with gold." They realized that no other cow would do; they had to have it at any price. They agreed to buy the cow and paid with its skin filled with gold.

The Quran says, And recall when Musa said to his people, "God commands you to sacrifice a heifer." They said, "Do you make a mockery of us?" He said, "God forbid that I should be so ignorant."

They said, "Call upon your Lord to show us which one." He said, "He says she is a heifer, neither too old, nor too young, but in between. So do what you are commanded." They said, "Call upon your Lord to show us what her color is." He said, "He says she is a yellow heifer, bright in color, pleasing to the beholders."

They said, "Call upon your Lord to show us which one; the heifers look alike to us; and God willing, we will be guided." He said, "He says she is a heifer, neither yoked to plow the earth, nor to irrigate the field; sound without blemish." They said, "Now you have brought the truth." So they slew her; though they almost did not.

> And recall when you killed a person, and disputed in the matter; but God was to expose what you were hiding. We said, "Strike him with part of it." Thus God brings the dead to life; and He shows you His signs, that you may understand.
>
> Then after that your hearts hardened. They were as rocks, or even harder. For there are some rocks from which rivers gush out, and others that splinter and water comes out from them, and others that sink in awe of God. God is not unaware of what you do. (2:67-74)

وَإِذْ قَالَ مُوسَىٰ لِقَوْمِهِ إِنَّ ٱللَّهَ يَأْمُرُكُمْ أَن تَذْبَحُوا۟ بَقَرَةً قَالُوٓا۟ أَتَتَّخِذُنَا هُزُوًا قَالَ أَعُوذُ بِٱللَّهِ أَنْ أَكُونَ مِنَ ٱلْجَٰهِلِينَ ٦٧ قَالُوا۟ ٱدْعُ لَنَا رَبَّكَ يُبَيِّن لَّنَا مَا هِيَ قَالَ إِنَّهُ يَقُولُ إِنَّهَا بَقَرَةٌ لَّا فَارِضٌ وَلَا بِكْرٌ عَوَانٌ بَيْنَ ذَٰلِكَ فَٱفْعَلُوا۟ مَا تُؤْمَرُونَ ٦٨ قَالُوا۟ ٱدْعُ لَنَا رَبَّكَ يُبَيِّن لَّنَا مَا لَوْنُهَا قَالَ إِنَّهُ يَقُولُ إِنَّهَا بَقَرَةٌ صَفْرَآءُ فَاقِعٌ لَّوْنُهَا تَسُرُّ ٱلنَّٰظِرِينَ ٦٩ قَالُوا۟ ٱدْعُ لَنَا رَبَّكَ يُبَيِّن لَّنَا مَا هِيَ إِنَّ ٱلْبَقَرَ تَشَٰبَهَ عَلَيْنَا وَإِنَّا إِن شَآءَ ٱللَّهُ لَمُهْتَدُونَ ٧٠ قَالَ إِنَّهُ يَقُولُ إِنَّهَا بَقَرَةٌ لَّا ذَلُولٌ تُثِيرُ ٱلْأَرْضَ وَلَا تَسْقِى ٱلْحَرْثَ مُسَلَّمَةٌ لَّا شِيَةَ فِيهَا قَالُوا۟ ٱلْـَٰٔنَ جِئْتَ بِٱلْحَقِّ فَذَبَحُوهَا وَمَا كَادُوا۟ يَفْعَلُونَ ٧١ وَإِذْ قَتَلْتُمْ نَفْسًا فَٱدَّٰرَٰٔتُمْ فِيهَا وَٱللَّهُ مُخْرِجٌ مَّا كُنتُمْ تَكْتُمُونَ ٧٢ فَقُلْنَا ٱضْرِبُوهُ بِبَعْضِهَا كَذَٰلِكَ يُحْىِ ٱللَّهُ ٱلْمَوْتَىٰ وَيُرِيكُمْ ءَايَٰتِهِ لَعَلَّكُمْ تَعْقِلُونَ ٧٣ ثُمَّ قَسَتْ قُلُوبُكُم مِّنۢ بَعْدِ ذَٰلِكَ فَهِىَ كَٱلْحِجَارَةِ أَوْ أَشَدُّ قَسْوَةً وَإِنَّ مِنَ ٱلْحِجَارَةِ لَمَا يَتَفَجَّرُ مِنْهُ ٱلْأَنْهَٰرُ وَإِنَّ مِنْهَا لَمَا يَشَّقَّقُ فَيَخْرُجُ مِنْهُ ٱلْمَآءُ وَإِنَّ مِنْهَا لَمَا يَهْبِطُ مِنْ خَشْيَةِ ٱللَّهِ وَمَا ٱللَّهُ بِغَٰفِلٍ عَمَّا تَعْمَلُونَ ٧٤

(2:67-74)

The boy and his mother learned that Allah always provides sustenance. The desperation of the people looking for a specific cow also taught them that we do not always need to know the complete answer, and that answers come in due time.

Story of Al-Khidr and Musa:

One day Musa gave a very good speech that moved many people. Someone amongst them asked, "O Messenger of Allah, is there another man on earth more learned than you?"

Musa replied, "No!" because he believed that he was specially chosen by Allah to perform miracles and because Allah gave him the Torah. However, Allah revealed to Musa that no man could know all there is to know. And that one person cannot own all the knowledge of the world.

Allah sent Musa on a journey to teach him that there would always be another who knew what others did not. Musa asked Allah, "O Allah, where is this man? I would like to meet him and learn from him."

Allah told Musa that he would find the man by following these instructions: he had to take a live fish in a water filled boat; when the fish disappeared, he would find the man.

Musa left to go find the man. He went with a young man who carried the fish onto the boat. They reached a place where two rivers met and Musa decided to rest there. Musa fell asleep. While he was asleep, the other man saw the fish wriggle out of the boat, fall into the river, and swim away. However, when Musa woke up the man forgot to tell him. They continued their trip until finally the man remembered to tell him. Hearing the story about the fish swimming away, Musa said, "This is exactly what we are looking for!" So they retraced their steps back to the place where the rivers met and where the fish had jumped out. When they got there they found a man wearing a hood with his face covered. It was the man they were looking for. His name was Al-Khidr.

Musa greeted him, and said "I am Musa."
The man asked, "Musa of Bani Israel?"
Musa said, "Yes, I have come to you so that you may teach me from those things which Allah has taught you."
He said, "O Musa! I have some of the knowledge of Allah which Allah has taught me and which you do not know, and you have some of the knowledge of Allah which Allah has taught you and which I do not know."
Musa asked, "May I follow you?"
He said, "But you will not be able to remain patient with me, for how can you be patient about things which you will not be able to understand?"
Musa said, "You will find me truly patient, and I will not disobey you."

So the two of them set out walking along the seashore. A boat passed by them and they asked the people on the boat to take them on board with them. The people on board recognized Al-Khidr, so they took them on board without charging them any money. When they were on the boat, a sparrow came and stood on the edge of the boat and dipped its beak once or twice into the sea. Al-Khidr said to Musa, "O Musa! My knowledge and your knowledge have not decreased Allah's knowledge except as much as this sparrow has decreased the water of the sea with its beak." This meant that Allah's knowledge was much greater than theirs. Then suddenly Al-Khidr made a hole in the boat. Musa said to him, "What have you done? They took us on board charging us nothing; yet you have intentionally made a hole in their boat as to drown its passengers. You have done a dreadful thing!" Al-Khidr replied, "Did I not tell you that you would not be able to remain patient with me?" Musa replied: "Do not blame me for what I have forgotten, and do not be hard on me." So the first excuse of Musa was that he had forgotten.

When they left the boat and started walking on the land they passed by a group of boys playing. Al-Khidr took a hold of one of the boys and killed him. Musa said to him, "Have you killed an innocent person who has not killed any person? You have really done a horrible thing." Al-Khidr said again, "Did I not tell you that you could not remain patient with me?" Musa said, "If I ask you about anything after this, don't accompany me any longer. You have received an excuse from me."

Then both of them went on until they came to some people in a village. They asked the villagers for some food but the villagers refused. In this village there was a broken wall that was about to collapse. Al-Khidr fixed the wall just by touching it with his hands. Musa said, "These are the people whom we have called on for help, but they neither gave us food, nor entertained us as guests, yet you have repaired their wall without asking for anything in return."

Having been questioned many times by Musa, Al-Khidr said, "This is where we part, but I will tell you the explanation of those things on which you could not remain patient." He then explained, "As for the ship, it belonged to poor people working in the sea. So I wished to make a defective damage in it, because there was a king after them who seized by force every ship that was in good shape." If the boat was damaged, the king wouldn't take it and the people could repair it and continue using it.

And as for the boy, his parents were believers, and we knew he would give them a difficult time by rebelling. Allah had decreed that the boy would die.

Al-Khidr explained that his actions were based on wisdom from Allah, and Musa realized that there was often hidden wisdom in situations that seemed unfortunate.

"And as for the wall, Al-Khidr continued, "it belonged to two orphan boys in the village. And underneath the wall there was a treasure belonging to them. Their father was a righteous man, and Allah intended that when they grew up they would take out their treasure. This would ensure that the treasure would remain in safe keeping for the children."

The Quran says, Recall when Musa said to his servant, "I will not give up until I reach the junction of the two rivers, even if it takes me years." Then, when they reached the junction between them, they forgot about their fish. It found its way into the river, slipping away.

When they went further, he said to his servant, "Bring us our lunch; we were exposed in our travel to much fatigue."

He said, "Do you remember when we rested by the rock? I forgot about the fish. It was only the devil who made me forget it. And so it found its way to the river, amazingly." He said, "This is what we were seeking." And so they turned back retracing their steps. Then they came upon a servant of Ours, whom We had blessed with mercy from Us, and had taught him knowledge from Our Own.

Musa said to him, "May I follow you, so that you may teach me some of the guidance you were taught?" He said, "You will not be able to endure with me.

And how will you endure what you have no knowledge of?" He said, "If you follow me, do not ask me about anything, until I myself make mention of it to you." So they set out. Until, when they had boarded the boat, he holed it. He said, "Did you hole it, to drown its passengers? You have done something awful."

He said, "Did I not tell you that you will not be able to endure with me?" So they set out. Until, when they had boarded the boat, he holed it. He said, "Did you hole it, to drown its passengers? You have done something awful." He said, "Did I not tell you that you will not be able to endure with me?" He said, "Do not rebuke me for forgetting, and do not make my course difficult for me."

Then they set out. Until, when they encountered a boy, he killed him. He said, "Did you kill a pure soul, who killed no one? You have done something terrible." He said, "Did I not tell you that you will not be able to endure with me?" He said, "If I ask you about anything after this, then do not keep company with me. You have received excuses from me."

So they set out. Until, when they reached the people of a town, they asked them for food, but they refused to offer them hospitality. There they found a wall about to collapse, and he repaired it. He said, "If you wanted, you could have obtained a payment for it." He said, "This is the parting between you and me. I will tell you the interpretation of what you were unable to endure.

As for the boat, it belonged to paupers working at sea. I wanted to damage it because there was a king coming after them seizing every boat by force. As for the boy, his parents were believers, and we feared he would overwhelm them with oppression and disbelief. So we wanted their Lord to replace him with someone better in purity, and closer to mercy.

And as for the wall, it belonged to two orphaned boys in the town. Beneath it was a treasure that belonged to them. Their father was a righteous man. Your Lord wanted them to reach their maturity, and then extract their treasure-as a mercy from your Lord. I did not do it of my own accord. This is the interpretation of what you were unable to endure." (18:60-82)

وَإِذْ قَالَ مُوسَىٰ لِفَتَاهُ لَا أَبْرَحُ حَتَّىٰ أَبْلُغَ مَجْمَعَ ٱلْبَحْرَيْنِ أَوْ أَمْضِيَ حُقُبًا ٦٠ فَلَمَّا بَلَغَا مَجْمَعَ بَيْنِهِمَا نَسِيَا حُوتَهُمَا فَٱتَّخَذَ سَبِيلَهُ ۥ فِى ٱلْبَحْرِ سَرَبًا ٦١ فَلَمَّا جَاوَزَا قَالَ لِفَتَاهُ ءَاتِنَا غَدَاءَنَا لَقَدْ لَقِينَا مِن سَفَرِنَا هَٰذَا نَصَبًا ٦٢ قَالَ أَرَءَيْتَ إِذْ أَوَيْنَا إِلَى ٱلصَّخْرَةِ فَإِنِّى نَسِيتُ ٱلْحُوتَ وَمَا أَنسَانِيهُ إِلَّا ٱلشَّيْطَانُ أَنْ أَذْكُرَهُ ۥ وَٱتَّخَذَ سَبِيلَهُ ۥ فِى ٱلْبَحْرِ عَجَبًا ٦٣ قَالَ ذَٰلِكَ مَا كُنَّا نَبْغِ فَٱرْتَدَّا عَلَىٰ ءَاثَارِهِمَا قَصَصًا ٦٤ فَوَجَدَا عَبْدًا مِّنْ عِبَادِنَا ءَاتَيْنَٰهُ رَحْمَةً مِّنْ عِندِنَا وَعَلَّمْنَٰهُ مِن لَّدُنَّا عِلْمًا ٦٥ قَالَ لَهُ ۥ مُوسَىٰ هَلْ أَتَّبِعُكَ عَلَىٰٓ أَن تُعَلِّمَنِ مِمَّا عُلِّمْتَ رُشْدًا ٦٦ قَالَ إِنَّكَ لَن تَسْتَطِيعَ مَعِىَ صَبْرًا ٦٧ وَكَيْفَ تَصْبِرُ عَلَىٰ مَا لَمْ تُحِطْ بِهِۦ خُبْرًا ٦٨ قَالَ سَتَجِدُنِىٓ إِن شَاءَ ٱللَّهُ صَابِرًا وَلَا أَعْصِى لَكَ أَمْرًا ٦٩ قَالَ فَإِنِ ٱتَّبَعْتَنِى فَلَا تَسْـَٔلْنِى عَن شَىْءٍ حَتَّىٰٓ أُحْدِثَ لَكَ مِنْهُ ذِكْرًا ٧٠ فَٱنطَلَقَا حَتَّىٰٓ إِذَا رَكِبَا فِى ٱلسَّفِينَةِ خَرَقَهَا قَالَ أَخَرَقْتَهَا لِتُغْرِقَ أَهْلَهَا لَقَدْ جِئْتَ شَيْـًٔا إِمْرًا ٧١ قَالَ أَلَمْ أَقُلْ إِنَّكَ لَن تَسْتَطِيعَ مَعِىَ صَبْرًا ٧٢ قَالَ لَا تُؤَاخِذْنِى بِمَا نَسِيتُ وَلَا تُرْهِقْنِى مِنْ أَمْرِى عُسْرًا ٧٣ فَٱنطَلَقَا حَتَّىٰٓ إِذَا لَقِيَا غُلَٰمًا فَقَتَلَهُ ۥ قَالَ أَقَتَلْتَ نَفْسًا زَكِيَّةً بِغَيْرِ نَفْسٍ لَّقَدْ جِئْتَ شَيْـًٔا نُّكْرًا ٧٤ قَالَ أَلَمْ أَقُل لَّكَ إِنَّكَ لَن تَسْتَطِيعَ مَعِىَ صَبْرًا ٧٥ قَالَ إِن سَأَلْتُكَ عَن شَىْءٍ بَعْدَهَا فَلَا تُصَٰحِبْنِى قَدْ بَلَغْتَ مِن لَّدُنِّى عُذْرًا ٧٦ فَٱنطَلَقَا حَتَّىٰٓ إِذَآ أَتَيَآ أَهْلَ قَرْيَةٍ ٱسْتَطْعَمَآ أَهْلَهَا فَأَبَوْا أَن يُضَيِّفُوهُمَا فَوَجَدَا فِيهَا جِدَارًا يُرِيدُ أَن يَنقَضَّ فَأَقَامَهُ ۥ قَالَ لَوْ شِئْتَ لَتَّخَذْتَ عَلَيْهِ أَجْرًا ٧٧ قَالَ هَٰذَا فِرَاقُ بَيْنِى وَبَيْنِكَ سَأُنَبِّئُكَ بِتَأْوِيلِ مَا لَمْ تَسْتَطِع عَّلَيْهِ صَبْرًا ٧٨ أَمَّا ٱلسَّفِينَةُ فَكَانَتْ لِمَسَٰكِينَ يَعْمَلُونَ فِى ٱلْبَحْرِ فَأَرَدتُّ أَنْ أَعِيبَهَا وَكَانَ وَرَاءَهُم مَّلِكٌ يَأْخُذُ كُلَّ سَفِينَةٍ غَصْبًا ٧٩ وَأَمَّا ٱلْغُلَٰمُ فَكَانَ أَبَوَاهُ مُؤْمِنَيْنِ فَخَشِينَآ أَن يُرْهِقَهُمَا طُغْيَٰنًا وَكُفْرًا ٨٠ فَأَرَدْنَآ أَن يُبْدِلَهُمَا رَبُّهُمَا خَيْرًا مِّنْهُ زَكَوٰةً وَأَقْرَبَ رُحْمًا ٨١ وَأَمَّا ٱلْجِدَارُ فَكَانَ لِغُلَٰمَيْنِ يَتِيمَيْنِ فِى ٱلْمَدِينَةِ وَكَانَ تَحْتَهُ ۥ كَنزٌ لَّهُمَا وَكَانَ أَبُوهُمَا صَٰلِحًا فَأَرَادَ رَبُّكَ أَن يَبْلُغَآ أَشُدَّهُمَا وَيَسْتَخْرِجَا كَنزَهُمَا رَحْمَةً مِّن رَّبِّكَ وَمَا فَعَلْتُهُ ۥ عَنْ أَمْرِى ذَٰلِكَ تَأْوِيلُ مَا لَمْ تَسْطِع عَّلَيْهِ صَبْرًا ٨٢

(18:60-82)

EXERCISES:

1 Describe in your own words the lessons learned from the story of the boy and the cow

2 Describe in your own words the lessons learned from the story of Al-Khidr and Musa.

CONCLUSION

A hadith states that when Prophet Mohamed (pbuh) was given trouble by his people, he would say "'May Allah bestow His Mercy on Musa, for he was harmed more (in a worse manner) than this; yet he endured patiently.'" (Sahih Al-Bukhari)

Musa did, in fact, suffer greatly during his life and endured so much for the sake of Allah.

The Quran says, O you who believe! Do not be like those who abused Musa; but God cleared him of what they said. He was distinguished with God. (33:69)

يَـٰٓأَيُّهَا ٱلَّذِينَ ءَامَنُوا۟ لَا تَكُونُوا۟ كَٱلَّذِينَ ءَاذَوْا۟ مُوسَىٰ فَبَرَّأَهُ ٱللَّهُ مِمَّا قَالُوا۟ وَكَانَ عِندَ ٱللَّهِ وَجِيهًا ٦٩ (33:69)

Harun died shortly before Musa. His people were still wandering in the desert when he died.

The perseverance of Musa and Harun teaches us to see beyond closed doors and seemingly impossible situations. Their story teaches us to see Allah's mercy and to rely on His guidance.

The stories of Musa's life demonstrate his strong faith and Allah's promise and dedication to his role as a messenger to his people.

MUSA DIED WHILE HE WAS CONTENT.
HE HAD A RIGHTEOUS AND
FAITHFUL HEART.

EXERCISES:

Internet Activity: Watch the movie *Prince of Egypt.*
Compare and contrast the movie *Prince of Egypt* to the information in this book.

EXERCISE ANSWERS

Chapter 1:
1. Israelites are members of the tribes of Israel, which refer to the decedents of Prophet Yacub. Their original residence was a city named Canaan but they spread all around the Near East including Egypt.
2. Surah 28 Al Qassas - The Stories
3. More than 400
4. Asiyah, Pharaoh's wife
5. He put a burning coal in his mouth during a test from Pharaoh.
6. His sister told Pharaoh that she knew a woman that could feed Musa.

Chapter 2:
1. No
2. Self control. Resistance. Realized that he had acted excessively and emotionally and he prayed for Allah's forgiveness. He knew that exceeding legitimate limits might turn the defender into an assaulter, and the initial assaulter into a victim. He now firmly believed that he will never support evildoing regardless of the party to which you belong. He also learned that there is fine line between reasonable and legitimate defense and in overstepping authority.
3. Median.
4. 10 years.

Chapter 3:

1. A fire.
2. Turning his stick into a snake and turning his hand to shining white.
3. For his brother to help him in Egypt.
4. Because he had better speech.

Chapter 4:

1. Showing lack of respect, not friendly, distant.
2. Imprisonment.
3. They named them wizards and imprisoned them.
4. Musa asked the magicians to perform first. They threw their magical objects down on the ground. Their stick and ropes took the forms of wriggling serpents while the crowd watched in amazement. Pharaoh and his men applauded loudly. Then Musa threw his stick. It began to wriggle and became an enormous snake. The people stood up to see better. Pharaoh and his men sat quietly as, one by one, Musa's huge snake swallowed all the other smaller snakes. Musa bent to pick it up, and it became a stick again in his hand. The crowd stood up shouting and screaming with excitement. A wonder like this had never been seen before! When the magicians saw this they prostrated themselves to Allah, declaring: "We believe in the Lord of Musa and Harun." Pharaoh grew very angry and began planning his next move. He accused the magicians and Musa of secretly arranging the stunt. He demanded that the magicians confess to their scheme, threatening them with death. They refused and stuck to their new belief. No longer hiding his cruel nature, Pharaoh threatened to cut off their hands and feet and to crucify them on the trunks of palm trees as an example to his subjects.

Chapter 5:

1. Drought, flood, locusts, frogs, blood in the water
2. A large grasshopper with strong power of flight.
3. Break a promise.
4. 5

Chapter 6:

1. When they reached the impassable beach.
2. The water collapsed on them.
3. In your own words.

Chapter 7:

1. A hard time
2. Sinai
3. Musa received the 10 commandments.
4. 1. Join not anything in worship with Allah (Shirk) 2. Be good and dutiful to parents. 3. Kill not your children because of poverty. 4. Come not near to "shameful" sins whether committed openly or secretly. 5. Kill not anyone whom Allah has forbidden. 6. Come not near to the orphan's property, except to improve it, until he (or she) attains the age of full strength.
7. Give full measure and full weight with justice. 8. Whenever you speak, say the truth even if a near relative is concerned. 9. Fulfill the Covenant of Allah. 10. And, indeed, this is My Straight Path, so follow it, and do not follow other paths, for they will separate you away from His Path. This He has ordained for you that you may become pious.

Chapter 8:

1. He saw all the people singing, dancing and worshiping a calf.
2. To ask forgiveness from Allah.
3. He tried but they were out of control.

Chapter 9:

1. In your own words.
2. In your own words.

The Holy Quran text:
Quranexplorer.com